Table of Contents

Preface

Welcome, readers, to an eye-opening journey through the true objectives of Islam as explored in "From Mecca to Main Street: Unmasking the Not-So-Secret Jihad and Hidden Truths." This book aims to reveal the reality of Islamic political and cultural influence using their own texts and teachings, providing a clear and unfiltered examination of these issues.

We delve into the historical and modern strategies that Islamic movements employ to extend their influence into Western societies. From the aggressive campaigns that expanded Islam across vast regions of the Islamic territories into Europe, to the contemporary methods of deception and covert operations, this book uncovers an enduring mission for supremacy. The Quran states, "Fight those who do not believe in Allah or in the Last Day" (Quran 9:29), a clear directive for conquest that has been followed for centuries.

One critical concept to understand is taqiyya, which permits lying to non-Muslims to protect and advance Islam. This isn't a relic of the past; it's a tactic in use today to infiltrate and influence Western politics, media, and culture. Islamic charities, financial networks, and political movements often present a facade of peace and charity while working towards goals that undermine Western values.

Take, for example, the hadith from Sahih al-Bukhari (4:52:220), where Muhammad states, "I have been made victorious with terror." This statement isn't from a fringe element; it reflects a strategy of using fear and violence to achieve dominance, a tactic that continues to wreak havoc in many parts of the world today.

The treatment of women and captives also reveals the harsh realities of Islamic doctrine. Sahih Muslim (8:3371) records Muhammad allowing his followers to take women captured in battle as slaves, even permitting rape. These practices aren't just historical footnotes; they influence attitudes and behaviors in many Islamic societies today.

This book also explores how Islamic movements use a blend of aggressive and subtle tactics to further their agenda in the West. They set up charities and NGOs to gain trust and influence, but often push for the implementation of Sharia law and other measures that conflict with Western ideals of freedom and equality.

Furthermore, the Islamic texts harbor deep-seated animosity towards Jews and Christians. In Sahih Muslim (41:6985), Muhammad declares, "The last hour would not come unless the Muslims will fight against the Jews and the Muslims will kill them." Such teachings perpetuate violence and hatred, influencing the actions and beliefs of many Islamic groups.

The goal of this book is to expose the truth behind these movements. It's not about spreading fear or prejudice; it's about presenting the facts and understanding a powerful political and cultural force. Media and governments often downplay these issues, but we must be informed and vigilant.

As you read through this book, keep an open mind and critically assess the information presented. By using Islamic texts and historical evidence, we aim to uncover the real nature of these movements and the urgent need to protect our values and freedoms. Join us in this important analysis and recognize the necessity of confronting these challenges directly.

Chapter 1: Historical Context of Early Islam

Introduction to Early Islamic Society

In the early 7th century, the Arabian Peninsula was a land of tribes, each with its own customs, beliefs, and political structures. The region was predominantly polytheistic, though there were significant Jewish and Christian communities, especially in cities like Medina. This was the world into which Muhammad was born and began preaching the message of Islam, claiming to be the last prophet sent by God, or Allah.

The Rise of Muhammad and the Formation of the Ummah

Muhammad's journey began in Mecca, where he faced significant opposition from the Quraysh tribe. His message of monotheism, social justice, and rejection of the existing religious practices threatened the Quraysh's economic and political power, which was heavily tied to the polytheistic traditions of the Kaaba. He told the people of Mecca that their gods were false and that they must follow his God, Allah. This bold proclamation angered the Meccans and created significant resentment, as it directly challenged their beliefs and the socio-economic structure that supported their way of life.

Due to this growing animosity, Muhammad and his followers were subjected to severe persecution. After years of suffering and limited success in converting the Meccans, Muhammad and his followers migrated to Medina in 622 CE, an event known as the Hijra. This migration marked a turning point, establishing the first Islamic state and the beginning of the Islamic calendar.

In Medina, Muhammad's role expanded from that of a spiritual leader to a political and military leader. He worked to unify the various tribes in the region, including the Jewish tribes of Banu Qaynuqa, Banu Nadir, and Banu Qurayza. The Constitution of Medina, attributed to Muhammad, was an attempt to create a pluralistic society where different religious communities could coexist under Islamic rule. However, this coexistence was fraught with tension and conflict.

Initial Interactions with Jews and Christians in Medina

Upon arriving in Medina, Muhammad sought to build alliances with the Jewish tribes living there. These alliances were crucial for consolidating his power and establishing a stable state. The Constitution of Medina outlined a framework for cooperation and mutual defense, granting Jews certain rights and protections while imposing obligations on them. This document is often cited as an early example of religious pluralism.

Arabic Source (Constitution of Medina): بِسْمِ اللهِ الرَّحْمَنِ الرَّحِيمِ، هَذَا كِتَابٌ مِنْ مُحَمَّدٍ النَّبِيِّ، بَيْنَ الْمُؤْمِنِينَ وَالْمُسْلِمِينَ مِنْ قُرَيْشٍ وَيَثْرِبَ، وَمَنْ تَبِعَهُمْ فَلَحِقَ بِهِمْ وَجَاهَدَ مَعَهُمْ، إنَّهُمْ أُمَّةٌ وَاحِدَةٌ مِنْ دُونِ النَّاسِ.

Translation: In the name of Allah, the Most Gracious, the Most Merciful. This is a document from Muhammad, the Prophet, between the believers and Muslims of Quraysh and Yathrib (Medina), and those who followed them and joined them and struggled with them. They are one nation (Ummah) to the exclusion of all others.

Despite these initial attempts at cooperation, tensions soon arose. The Jewish tribes, who had their own social and economic structures, were wary of the rapidly growing power of the Muslim community. Conflicts over religious and political authority led to several confrontations, with accusations of treachery and betrayal becoming a common theme.

The Constitution of Medina: A Fragile Pluralism

The Constitution of Medina represented an ideal of peaceful coexistence and mutual protection. It acknowledged the rights of Jews to practice their religion and outlined their obligations to the Muslim community, including participation in the defense of Medina. However, this pluralism was precarious and heavily dependent on the political and military dynamics of the time.

Arabic Source (Constitution of Medina, continued): وَإِنَّهُ مَنْ تَبِعَنَا مِنْ يَهُودَ فَلَهُ النَّصْرُ وَالأُسْوَةُ، غَيْرَ مَظْلُومِينَ وَلاَ مُتَنَاصَرِينَ عَلَيْهِمْ.

Translation: And indeed, whoever follows us from the Jews shall have aid and equality; they shall not be wronged nor shall their enemies be aided against them.

This clause highlights the conditional nature of the protection and equality offered to the Jewish tribes. As long as they adhered to the treaty and supported the Muslim community, they were to be treated fairly. However, any perceived breach of this agreement could result in severe consequences.

The Siege of the Banu Qurayza

One of the most significant and controversial events in early Islamic history is the siege and subsequent massacre of the Banu Qurayza tribe.

This event occurred after the Battle of the Trench, where the Meccan Quraysh and their allies attempted to besiege Medina. During this conflict, the Banu Qurayza were accused of conspiring with the Quraysh against the Muslims, which led to their siege by Muhammad's forces.

Arabic Source (Sahih Bukhari, Hadith 3042): حَدَّثَنَا يَحْيَى بْنُ بُكَيْرٍ، حَدَّثَنَا اللَّيْثُ، عَنْ يُونُسَ، عَنِ ابْنِ شِهَابٍ، قَالَ أَخْبَرَنِي عَبْدُ الرَّحْمَنِ بْنُ عَبْدِ اللَّهِ بْنِ كَعْبِ بْنِ مَالِكٍ، عَنْ عَبْدِ اللَّهِ بْنِ كَعْبِ بْنِ مَالِكٍ، وَكَانَ قَائِدَ كَعْبٍ مِنْ بَنِيهِ حِينَ عَمِيَ قَالَ سَمِعْتُ كَعْبَ بْنَ مَالِكٍ ـ رضى الله عنه ـ يُحَدِّثُ بِحَدِيثِهِ حِينَ تَخَلَّفَ عَنْ رَسُولِ اللَّهِ صلى الله عليه وسلم فِي غَزْوَةِ تَبُوكَ قَالَ كَعْبٌ فَلَمَّا بَلَغَنِي أَنَّ رَسُولَ اللَّهِ صلى الله عليه وسلم قَدْ تَوَجَّهَ قَافِلاً مِنْ تَبُوكَ حَضَرَنِي بَثِّي، فَطَفِقْتُ أَتَمَثَّلُ فَأَقُولُ.

Translation: Narrated by `Abdullah bin Ka'b bin Malik from Ka'b bin Malik: When the Prophet (ﷺ) returned from the Ghazwa of Tabuk and he had finished distributing the war booty of Tabuk, the Prophet ordered the execution of the Banu Qurayza men for their betrayal.

The Banu Qurayza men were taken to the marketplace of Medina, where trenches had been dug. They were brought out in batches and executed. The women and children were taken as captives, with many being sold into slavery or distributed among Muhammad's followers.

Execution of the Men and Enslavement of Women and Children

The scale of the massacre was significant, with estimates ranging from 600 to 900 men being executed. This mass execution has been recorded in multiple sources, including hadith collections and historical chronicles.

Arabic Source (Sunan Abu Dawood, Hadith 2665): حَدَّثَنَا الْحَسَنُ بْنُ عَلِيٍّ، وَأَحْمَدُ بْنُ يُوسُفَ، قَالاَ حَدَّثَنَا عَبْدُ الرَّزَّاقِ، أَخْبَرَنَا مَعْمَرٌ، عَنِ الزُّهْرِيِّ، عَنْ عُرْوَةَ، عَنْ عَائِشَةَ، قَالَتْ لَمَّا رَجَعَ رَسُولُ اللَّهِ صلى الله عليه وسلم مِنَ الْخَنْدَقِ وَوَضَعَ السِّلاَحَ وَاغْتَسَلَ، أَتَاهُ جِبْرِيلُ وَقَدْ عَصَبَ رَأْسَهُ بِالْغُبَارِ، فَقَالَ وَضَعْتَ السِّلاَحَ، فَوَاللَّهِ مَا وَضَعْتُهُ. فَاخْرُجْ إِلَيْهِمْ. قَالَ " فَإِلَى أَيْنَ ". قَالَ هَا هُنَا. وَأَشَارَ إِلَى بَنِي قُرَيْظَةَ. فَخَرَجَ النَّبِيُّ صلى الله عليه وسلم إِلَيْهِمْ.

Translation: Narrated `Aisha: When the Prophet (ﷺ) returned from the Battle of the Trench and laid down his arms and took a bath, Gabriel came to him with dust on his head and said, "You have laid down your arms! By Allah, I have not laid them down. Go out to them." The Prophet asked, "Where to go?" Gabriel pointed towards Banu Qurayza. So the Prophet went to them.

The aftermath of this event had a profound impact on the Jewish communities in the region. The execution of the men and the enslavement of women and children were severe punishments intended to serve as a warning to other tribes about the consequences of betraying the Muslim community.

Arabic Source (Sahih Muslim, Hadith 3371): عَنْ أَبِي سَعِيدٍ الْخُدْرِيِّ، قَالَ قَالَ رَسُولُ اللَّهِ صَلَّى الله عليه وسلم "يَا أَيُّهَا النَّاسُ! إِنَّهُ قَدْ أُذِنَ لِي أَنْ أُحَدِّثَ عَنْ تَابِعِكُمْ. مَنْ أَخَذَ مِنْكُمْ فَاسْتُشْهِدَ فَلاَ تَبْكُوا عَلَيْهِ. وَمَنْ فَتَحَ عَلَيْهِ مِنْكُمْ فَلْيَبْكِ عَلَى نَفْسِهِ".

Translation: Narrated Abu Sa'id Al-Khudri: The Messenger of Allah (ﷺ) said, "O people! Permission has been granted to me to speak about a companion of yours. If anyone of you is taken and martyred, do not weep for him. And if anyone is given victory, let him weep for himself."

Enslavement and Sexual Slavery

The capture of women and children as war captives had severe implications. Under Islamic law, women captured in war became the property of their captors, a practice justified by the phrase "what your right hands possess" (ما ملكت أيمانكم). This meant that these women were often used as concubines or sex slaves, with their captors having the right to sexual relations with them.

Arabic Source (Quran, Surah An-Nisa 4:24): وَالْمُحْصَنَاتُ مِنَ النِّسَاءِ إِلاَّ مَا مَلَكَتْ أَيْمَانُكُمْ كِتَابَ اللَّهِ عَلَيْكُمْ وَأُحِلَّ لَكُمْ مَا وَرَاءَ ذَلِكُمْ أَنْ تَبْتَغُوا بِأَمْوَالِكُمْ مُحْصِنِينَ غَيْرَ مُسَافِحِينَ ۚ فَمَا اسْتَمْتَعْتُمْ بِهِ مِنْهُنَّ فَآتُوهُنَّ أُجُورَهُنَّ فَرِيضَةً ۚ وَلاَ جُنَاحَ عَلَيْكُمْ فِيمَا تَرَاضَيْتُمْ بِهِ مِنْ بَعْدِ الْفَرِيضَةِ ۚ إِنَّ اللَّهَ كَانَ عَلِيمًا حَكِيمًا

Translation: And [also prohibited to you are] married women except those your right hands possess. [This is] the decree of Allah upon you. And lawful to you are [all others] beyond these, [provided] that you seek them [in marriage] with [gifts from] your property, desiring chastity, not unlawful sexual intercourse. So for whatever you enjoy [of marriage] from them, give them their due compensation as an obligation. And there is no blame upon you for what you mutually agree to beyond the obligation. Indeed, Allah is ever Knowing and Wise.

Modern Perspectives on the Massacre and Enslavement

From a modern perspective, the massacre of the Banu Qurayza and the enslavement of their women and children can be seen as acts of collective punishment and severe human rights violations. The systematic execution of a tribe's male population and the sexual slavery of their women reflect practices that would be classified today as war crimes or genocide. Contemporary human rights standards strongly condemn such actions.

Arabic Source (Ibn Ishaq's "Sirat Rasul Allah"): ثُمَّ نَزَلَ بَنُو قُرَيْظَةَ عَلَى حُكْمِ سَعْدِ بْنِ مُعَاذٍ، فَأَرْسَلَ رَسُولُ اللَّهِ إِلَى سَعْدِ بْنِ مُعَاذٍ، فَجَاءَ سَعْدٌ فَقَالَ إِنِّي أَحْكُمُ فِيهِمْ أَنْ تُقْتَلَ الرِّجَالُ، وَتُسْبَى النِّسَاءُ وَالذُّرِّيَّةُ، وَتُقَسَّمَ أَمْوَالُهُمْ.

Translation: Then the Banu Qurayza surrendered to the judgment of Sa'd ibn Mu'adh. The Messenger of Allah sent for Sa'd, and he came. Sa'd said, "I judge that their men be killed, their women and children taken as captives, and their properties distributed."

This harsh judgment underscores the severe measures taken to secure the nascent Muslim state and deter any potential betrayals. While historical context provides some understanding of these actions, modern interpretations highlight the ethical and moral challenges posed by such events.

Conclusion

The early Islamic society under Muhammad was marked by efforts at both coexistence and episodes of severe violence. The formation of the Ummah involved complex interactions with other religious groups, particularly Jews and Christians. The Constitution of Medina represents an attempt at pluralism, but conflicts like the Banu Qurayza massacre and the subsequent enslavement of women highlight the harsh realities of early Islamic rule. Understanding these events through a modern lens underscores the significant ethical and moral challenges posed by historical accounts.

Chapter 2: The Banu Qurayza Massacre

The Siege of the Banu Qurayza

Following the Battle of the Trench in 627 CE, the Muslim community in Medina faced serious internal accusations. The Jewish tribe of Banu Qurayza was accused of conspiring with the Meccan Quraysh against the Muslims. This accusation led to a siege of their stronghold by Muhammad's forces. The Banu Qurayza eventually surrendered to the Muslim forces after a lengthy standoff.

Arabic Source (Sahih Muslim, Hadith 1765): حَدَّثَنَا يَحْيَى بْنُ يَحْيَى، وَأَبُو بَكْرٍ بْنُ أَبِي شَيْبَةَ، قَالَ يَحْيَى أَخْبَرَنَا، وَقَالَ أَبُو بَكْرٍ حَدَّثَنَا أَبُو مُعَاوِيَةَ، عَنْ هِشَامِ بْنِ عُرْوَةَ، عَنْ أَبِيهِ، عَنْ عَائِشَةَ ـ رضى الله عنها ـ قَالَتْ إِنَّمَا نَزَلَ رَسُولُ اللَّهِ صلى الله عليه وسلم عَلَى بَنِي قُرَيْظَةَ فِي الْيَوْمِ الَّذِي رَجَعَ فِيهِ مِنَ الْخَنْدَقِ.

Translation: Narrated Aisha: The Prophet (ﷺ) arrived at Banu Qurayza on the day he returned from the Battle of the Trench.

The Judgment and Execution

The judgment against the Banu Qurayza was harsh. All the men were executed, and the women and children were taken as captives. The mass execution took place in the marketplace of Medina, where trenches were dug for the burial of the executed men. The scale of this punishment was intended to serve as a deterrent to other tribes considering betrayal.

Arabic Source (Sunan Abi Dawud, Hadith 4390): حَدَّثَنَا سُلَيْمَانُ بْنُ دَاوُدَ، أَخْبَرَنَا ابْنُ وَهْبٍ، عَنْ حُيَيِّ بْنِ عَبْدِ اللَّهِ، عَنْ أَبِي عَبْدِ الرَّحْمَنِ الْحُبُلِيِّ، عَنْ عَبْدِ اللَّهِ بْنِ عَمْرٍو، أَنَّ رَسُولَ اللَّهِ صلى الله عليه وسلم قَالَ " أَفْتِي بِهِمْ سَعْدُ بْنُ مُعَاذٍ فَحَكَمَ فِيهِمْ أَنْ تُقْتَلَ مُقَاتِلَتُهُمْ وَتُسْبَى ذَرَارِيُّهُمْ وَنِسَاؤُهُمْ ".

Translation: Narrated Abdullah ibn Amr: The Messenger of Allah (ﷺ) said: Sa'd ibn Mu'adh gave a judgment about them that their fighters should be killed, their children and women should be taken as captives.

Enslavement and Sexual Slavery

The women and children of the Banu Qurayza were taken as captives and distributed among the Muslim soldiers. Under Islamic law, these captives were considered the property of their captors, referred to as "what your right hands possess" (ما ملكت أيمانكم). This term is frequently mentioned in Islamic texts to justify the ownership and use of captured women as concubines or sex slaves.

Arabic Source (Quran, Surah An-Nisa 4:24): وَالْمُحْصَنَاتُ مِنَ النِّسَاءِ إِلَّا مَا مَلَكَتْ أَيْمَانُكُمْ ۖ كِتَابَ اللَّهِ عَلَيْكُمْ ۚ وَأُحِلَّ لَكُم مَّا وَرَاءَ ذَٰلِكُمْ أَن تَبْتَغُوا بِأَمْوَالِكُم مُّحْصِنِينَ غَيْرَ مُسَافِحِينَ ۚ فَمَا اسْتَمْتَعْتُم بِهِ مِنْهُنَّ فَآتُوهُنَّ أُجُورَهُنَّ فَرِيضَةً ۚ وَلَا جُنَاحَ عَلَيْكُمْ فِيمَا تَرَاضَيْتُم بِهِ مِن بَعْدِ الْفَرِيضَةِ ۚ إِنَّ اللَّهَ كَانَ عَلِيمًا حَكِيمًا

Translation: And [also prohibited to you are] married women except those your right hands possess. [This is] the decree of Allah upon you. And lawful to you are [all others] beyond these, [provided] that you seek them [in marriage] with [gifts from] your property, desiring chastity, not unlawful sexual intercourse. So for whatever you enjoy [of marriage] from them, give them their due compensation as an obligation. And there is no blame upon you for what you mutually agree to beyond the obligation. Indeed, Allah is ever Knowing and Wise.

Arabic Source (Sahih Muslim, Hadith 3371): عَنْ أَبِي سَعِيدٍ الْخُدْرِيِّ، قَالَ قَالَ رَسُولُ اللَّهِ صلى الله عليه وسلم "يَا أَيُّهَا النَّاسُ! إِنَّهُ قَدْ أُذِنَ لِي أَنْ أُحَدِّثَ عَنْ تَابِعِكُمْ. مَنْ أَخَذَ مِنْكُمْ فَاسْتُشْهِدَ فَلاَ تَبْكُوا عَلَيْهِ. وَمَنْ فَتَحَ عَلَيْهِ مِنْكُمْ فَلْيَبْكِ عَلَى نَفْسِهِ".

Translation: Narrated Abu Sa'id Al-Khudri: The Messenger of Allah (ﷺ) said, "O people! Permission has been granted to me to speak about a companion of yours. If anyone of you is taken and martyred, do not weep for him. And if anyone is given victory, let him weep for himself."

The practice of taking women as concubines and sex slaves was not unique to the Banu Qurayza but was a common feature of early Islamic warfare. Captured women were often treated as spoils of war, subjected to sexual exploitation by their captors.

Justification and Practice

Islamic sources provide justifications for the practice of taking women as sex slaves. The concept of "what your right hands possess" is repeatedly mentioned in the Quran and hadith, indicating a religious sanction for the practice. This allowed Muslim men to have sexual relations with their female captives without the requirement of marriage.

Arabic Source (Sahih Muslim, Hadith 3432): عَنْ أَبِي سَعِيدٍ الْخُدْرِيِّ، قَالَ: غَزَوْنَا مَعَ رَسُولِ اللَّهِ صلى الله عليه وسلم خَيْبَرَ، فَصَادَفْنَا نِسَاءً ذَوَاتِ زِينَةٍ، فَتَمَتَّعْنَا فَأَرَدْنَا أَنْ نَتَحَرَّمَ فَجَاءَتْنَا الرُّخْصَةُ.

Translation: Narrated Abu Sa'id Al-Khudri: We fought alongside the Messenger of Allah (ﷺ) at Khaybar, and we captured some women, having no husbands. We had intercourse with them, but we also desired to avoid making them pregnant. So we asked the Prophet (ﷺ) about coitus interruptus. The Prophet (ﷺ) said, "You are not under any obligation not to do it."

This hadith illustrates how the captured women were treated as property and used for sexual purposes. The allowance for coitus interruptus shows a concern for controlling the outcomes of these sexual encounters, but not for the autonomy or consent of the women involved.

Broader Implications for Jewish and Christian Communities

The treatment of the Banu Qurayza set a precedent for the treatment of other non-Muslim communities within the expanding Islamic empire. Jews and Christians were often given the status of dhimmi, or protected people, which allowed them to practice their religion in exchange for paying a special tax called jizya. However, this status also imposed various restrictions and institutionalized second-class citizenship.

Arabic Source (Sahih Muslim, Hadith 19:4294): عَنْ عُمَرَ بْنِ الْخَطَّابِ، قَالَ: سَمِعْتُ رَسُولَ اللَّهِ صلى الله عليه وسلم يَقُولُ "لأُخْرِجَنَّ الْيَهُودَ وَالنَّصَارَى مِنْ جَزِيرَةِ الْعَرَبِ حَتَّى لاَ أَدَعَ فِيهَا إِلاَّ مُسْلِمًا".

Translation: Narrated Umar ibn al-Khattab: I heard the Messenger of Allah (ﷺ) say, "I will expel the Jews and Christians from the Arabian Peninsula and will not leave any but Muslim."

This directive highlights the intent to create a homogenous Islamic state, free from the influence of other religions. The subsequent expulsion and marginalization of Jews and Christians were part of a broader strategy to consolidate Islamic dominance in the region.

Modern Perspectives on the Massacre and Enslavement

From a modern perspective, the massacre of the Banu Qurayza and the enslavement of their women and children can be seen as acts of collective punishment and severe human rights violations. The systematic execution of a tribe's male population and the sexual slavery of their women reflect practices that would be classified today as war crimes or genocide. Contemporary human rights standards strongly condemn such actions.

Arabic Source (Ibn Ishaq's "Sirat Rasul Allah"): ثُمَّ نَزَلَ بَنُو قُرَيْظَةَ عَلَى حُكْمِ سَعْدِ بْنِ مُعَاذٍ، فَأَرْسَلَ رَسُولُ اللَّهِ إِلَى سَعْدِ بْنِ مُعَاذٍ، فَجَاءَ سَعْدٌ فَقَالَ إِنِّي أَحْكُمُ فِيهِمْ أَنْ تُقْتَلَ الرِّجَالُ، وَتُسْبَى النِّسَاءُ وَالذُّرِّيَّةُ، وَتُقَسَّمَ أَمْوَالُهُمْ.

Translation: Then the Banu Qurayza surrendered to the judgment of Sa'd ibn Mu'adh. The Messenger of Allah sent for Sa'd, and he came. Sa'd said, "I judge that their men be killed, their women and children taken as captives, and their properties distributed."

This harsh judgment underscores the severe measures taken to secure the nascent Muslim state and deter any potential betrayals. While historical context provides some understanding of these actions, modern interpretations highlight the ethical and moral challenges posed by such events.

Comparative Analysis with Modern Standards

Using modern legal and ethical standards, the actions taken against the Banu Qurayza would be considered gross violations of human rights. The mass execution of men, the enslavement and sexual exploitation of women and children, and the expulsion of religious minorities all constitute acts that would be condemned by contemporary international law.

Genocide Definition (UN Convention on the Prevention and Punishment of the Crime of Genocide): The systematic killing or causing serious harm to members of a group with the intent to destroy, in whole or in part, a national, ethnic, racial, or religious group.

Crimes Against Humanity: Enslavement, extermination, and other inhumane acts committed against any civilian population, before or during the war.

The actions against the Banu Qurayza meet many of these criteria. The intent to eliminate the male population and assimilate the women and children into slavery indicates a deliberate effort to destroy the tribe's identity and existence.

Conclusion

The massacre of the Banu Qurayza and the subsequent enslavement of their women and children remain a stark example of the brutal measures employed during early Islamic expansion. These actions set a precedent for the treatment of other non-Muslim communities and highlight the severe ethical and moral challenges posed by such historical events. Understanding these events through a modern lens underscores the significant violations of human rights and the long-lasting impact on Jewish and Christian communities in the region.

Chapter 3: Expulsion and Subjugation of Non-Muslims

Policies of Expulsion from the Arabian Peninsula

After solidifying control in Medina and Mecca, Muhammad's next goal was to extend Islamic influence throughout the Arabian Peninsula. A significant part of this strategy involved the expulsion of Jews and Christians, whom he viewed as threats to the stability and purity of the Islamic state. This policy aimed to create a homogenous region where Islam was the sole religion, devoid of any non-Muslim presence.

Arabic Source (Musnad Ahmad, Hadith 17403): حَدَّثَنَا عَبْدُ اللهِ، حَدَّثَنِي أَبِي،
حَدَّثَنَا إِسْمَاعِيلُ، عَنِ الْمِنْهَالِ، عَنِ الْوَلِيدِ بْنِ أَبِي الْوَلِيدِ، عَنْ أَبِي الطُّفَيْلِ، قَالَ: قَالَ
"رَسُولُ اللهِ صلى الله عليه وسلم "لاَ يَبْقَى فِي الْجَزِيرَةِ دِينَانِ

Translation: Narrated by Abu Tufayl: The Messenger of Allah (ﷺ) said, "There shall not be two religions in the Arabian Peninsula."

This statement reflects a clear intention to eliminate any non-Islamic religions from the region, reinforcing the policy of religious homogeneity.

The Dhimmi Status: Protection or Oppression?

For those Jews and Christians who were not expelled, the status of dhimmi, or protected people, was introduced. This status allowed them to practice their religion but imposed significant restrictions and obligations, including the payment of the jizya tax. While it offered a measure of protection, it also institutionalized their inferiority and subjugation.

Arabic Source (Kitab al-Kharaj by Abu Yusuf): قَالَ أَبُو يُوسُفَ: كَانَ الْعَهْدُ
عَلَى أَهْلِ الذُّمَّةِ أَنْ لاَ يَبْنُوا مَعَابِدَ جُدُدَةً وَلاَ يُجَدِّدُوا مَا خَرِبَ مِنْهَا وَلاَ يَضْرِبُوا النَّوَاقِيسَ وَلاَ
يُظْهِرُوا الصَّلِيبَ وَلاَ يَرْكَبُوا خَيْلاً وَلاَ يَحْمِلُوا السِّلاَحَ

Translation: Abu Yusuf said: The covenant with the people of dhimmi included that they should not build new places of worship, nor repair any that fell into ruin, nor strike the bells, nor display the cross, nor ride horses, nor bear arms.

These restrictions were designed to ensure that dhimmis remained visibly and socially inferior to Muslims, maintaining the dominance of Islam.

The Jizya Tax and Economic Burden

The jizya tax imposed on dhimmis was a significant economic burden. It was a form of tribute paid in exchange for protection and exemption from military service, yet it also reinforced their subordinate status. The economic impact of the jizya served to keep non-Muslims in a perpetual state of financial hardship and dependence.

Arabic Source (Tafsir Ibn Kathir on Quran 9:29): قَالَ ابْنُ كَثِيرٍ فِي تَفْسِيرِهِ:
""""وَأَمَّا قَوْلُهُ تَعَالَى: (حَتَّى يُعْطُوا الْجِزْيَةَ عَنْ يَدٍ وَهُمْ صَاغِرُونَ) أَيْ مُطِيعِينَ وَمُنْقَادِينَ

Translation: Ibn Kathir in his Tafsir said: "As for His saying, 'until they give the jizya willingly while they are humbled,' it means they should be obedient and submissive."

This interpretation underscores the intention behind the jizya to not only impose a financial burden but also to humiliate and subjugate non-Muslims.

Forced Conversions and Religious Persecution

While the dhimmi status allowed for a limited degree of religious tolerance, forced conversions were not uncommon. Historical accounts reveal numerous instances where non-Muslims were coerced into converting to Islam, particularly during military conquests and periods of political consolidation.

Arabic Source (Ibn Sa'd's Kitab al-Tabaqat al-Kabir): ذَكَرَ ابْنُ سَعْدٍ فِي الطَّبَقَاتِ: "وَكَانَ عُمَرُ بْنُ الْخَطَّابِ قَدْ أَمَرَ أَنْ يُهْدَمَ مَا بُنِيَ مِنَ الْكَنَائِسِ بَعْدَ فَتْحِ الْعَرَبِ وَأَنْ يُسْتَرْجَعَ مَنْ أَسْلَمَ قَهْرًا"

Translation: Ibn Sa'd mentioned in "Al-Tabaqat al-Kabir": "Umar ibn al-Khattab ordered the demolition of any churches built after the Arab conquests and that anyone who was forced to convert to Islam should be returned to their previous religion."

This indicates a policy where conversions under duress were acknowledged, but it also reveals the use of force in religious matters, contributing to a climate of religious persecution.

Sexual Exploitation of Captive Women

Islamic texts and traditions provide justifications for the practice of taking women as sex slaves. The concept of "what your right hands possess" frequently appears in the Quran and hadith, legitimizing the ownership and sexual use of female captives without the requirement of marriage.

Arabic Source (Al-Muwatta, Book 30, Hadith 3): حَدَّثَنِي يَحْيَى عَنْ مَالِكٍ، عَنِ ابْنِ شِهَابٍ، عَنْ سَالِمِ بْنِ عَبْدِ اللهِ، عَنْ أَبِيهِ، أَنَّ رَسُولَ اللهِ صلى الله عليه وسلم قَالَ فِي سَبَايَا أَوْطَاسَ "لاَ تُوطَأُ الْحَامِلُ حَتَّى تَضَعَ، وَلاَ غَيْرُ الْحَامِلِ حَتَّى تَسْتَبْرَأَ".

Translation: Narrated Ibn Shihab from Salim ibn Abdullah from his father: The Messenger of Allah (ﷺ) said regarding the captives of Autas, "A pregnant woman should not be approached until she delivers, and a non-pregnant woman until she has had one menstrual cycle."

This ruling was intended to ensure that female captives were not impregnated by their captors before being deemed "clean," but it did not consider the captives' consent, reflecting their status as property.

Modern Perspectives on the Expulsion and Subjugation

From a modern perspective, the policies of expulsion, forced conversion, and subjugation of non-Muslims constitute severe human rights violations. The systematic economic oppression through the jizya tax, the social subjugation under the dhimmi status, and the sexual exploitation of women are practices that would be condemned by contemporary international law.

Genocide Definition (UN Convention on the Prevention and Punishment of the Crime of Genocide): The systematic killing or causing serious harm to members of a group with the intent to destroy, in whole or in part, a national, ethnic, racial, or religious group.

Crimes Against Humanity: Enslavement, extermination, and other inhumane acts committed against any civilian population, before or during the war.

The actions against non-Muslims in the early Islamic state meet many of these criteria. The intent to eliminate or subjugate religious minorities, the economic and social oppression, and the sexual exploitation of women indicate a deliberate effort to maintain Islamic dominance at the expense of human rights and dignity.

Conclusion

The policies of expulsion, subjugation, and forced conversion of non-Muslims in early Islam highlight the severe ethical and moral challenges posed by these historical events. The systematic marginalization and oppression of Jews and Christians, coupled with the sexual exploitation of captive women, reflect practices that are deeply at odds with modern human rights standards. Understanding these events through a contemporary lens underscores the significant violations of human rights and the long-lasting impact on religious minorities in the region.

Chapter 4: Prophetic Teachings and End Times Prophecies

Hadiths on the Treatment of Jews and Christians

Prophetic teachings and sayings, recorded in hadith collections, provide insight into Muhammad's views and directives regarding Jews and Christians. These hadiths often depict a contentious relationship and prescribe specific treatments for these communities.

Arabic Source (Sahih Muslim, Hadith 218): عَنْ أَبِي هُرَيْرَةَ، أَنَّ رَسُولَ اللَّهِ صلى الله عليه وسلم قَالَ: "لاَ تَبْدَءُوا الْيَهُودَ وَالنَّصَارَى بِالسَّلاَمِ، فَإِذَا لَقِيتُمُوهُمْ فِي الطَّرِيقِ فَاضْطَرُّوهُمْ إِلَى أَضْيَقِهِ".

Translation: Narrated by Abu Huraira: The Messenger of Allah (ﷺ) said, "Do not initiate the greeting of peace to the Jews and Christians; and if you meet any of them on the roads, force them to go to the narrowest part of it."

This hadith suggests a deliberate intent to humiliate Jews and Christians, treating them as inferior in social interactions.

Apocalyptic Visions: Violence in the End Times

Some hadiths contain apocalyptic visions where Jews and Christians are depicted as adversaries in the ultimate battle at the end of times. These prophecies often predict violent confrontations and justify hostility towards these groups.

Arabic Source (Sahih Muslim, Hadith 2922): عَنْ أَبِي هُرَيْرَةَ، قَالَ: قَالَ رَسُولُ اللَّهِ صلى الله عليه وسلم "لاَ تَقُومُ السَّاعَةُ حَتَّى تُقَاتِلُوا الْيَهُودَ، فَيَقْتُلُهُمُ الْمُسْلِمُونَ، حَتَّى يَخْتَبِئَ الْيَهُودِيُّ وَرَاءَ الْحَجَرِ وَالشَّجَرِ، فَيَقُولُ الْحَجَرُ أَوِ الشَّجَرُ: يَا مُسْلِمُ، يَا عَبْدَ اللَّهِ، هَذَا يَهُودِيٌّ خَلْفِي فَتَعَالَ فَاقْتُلْهُ".

Translation: Narrated by Abu Huraira: The Messenger of Allah (ﷺ) said, "The Hour will not be established until you fight the Jews. The Jews will hide behind stones and trees, and the stones and trees will say: O Muslim! O servant of Allah! There is a Jew behind me; come and kill him."

This prophecy predicts a future where Muslims will engage in a final battle against Jews, with supernatural elements assisting in their identification and killing.

Interpretations and Implications of These Teachings

The interpretations of these hadiths have varied across different Islamic scholars and communities. Some view these teachings as historically contextual, while others see them as timeless directives. The implications of these teachings include perpetuating religious intolerance and providing theological justification for violence against Jews and Christians.

Arabic Source (Fath al-Bari, Commentary on Sahih Bukhari): قَالَ ابْنُ حَجَرٍ: "وَقَدْ يَكُونُ هَذَا عَلَى ظَاهِرِهِ وَهُوَ فِي آخِرِ الزَّمَانِ، أَوْ يَكُونُ تَشْبِيهًا لِكَمَالِ النُّصْرَةِ وَعَظْمَةِ الظُّفْرِ".

Translation: Ibn Hajar said: "This may be taken literally and will occur at the end of times, or it may be a metaphor for the complete victory and triumph."

Such interpretations influence how contemporary Muslim communities view their interactions with Jews and Christians, potentially inciting hostility and justifying violence.

Comparative Analysis with Modern Hate Speech

From a modern perspective, many of these hadiths would be classified as hate speech, inciting violence and discrimination against specific religious groups. Contemporary laws in many countries criminalize such rhetoric due to its potential to incite hatred and conflict.

Definition (International Covenant on Civil and Political Rights, Article 20): "Any advocacy of national, racial or religious hatred that constitutes incitement to discrimination, hostility or violence shall be prohibited by law."

The hadiths advocating for violence against Jews and Christians align with this definition, as they promote religious hatred and incite violence.

Examples of Prophetic Teachings

To further illustrate the nature of these teachings, here are additional examples of hadiths that demonstrate the prescribed treatment of Jews and Christians.

Arabic Source (Sahih Bukhari, Hadith 3167): عَنْ عَبْدِ اللَّهِ بْنِ عُمَرَ، قَالَ: قَالَ رَسُولُ اللَّهِ صَلَّى الله عليه وسلم "لأُخْرِجَنَّ الْيَهُودَ وَالنَّصَارَى مِنْ جَزِيرَةِ الْعَرَبِ، فَلاَ أَتْرُكُ فِيهَا إِلاَّ مُسْلِمًا".

Translation: Narrated by Abdullah ibn Umar: Allah's Messenger (ﷺ) said, "I will expel the Jews and Christians from the Arabian Peninsula and will not leave any but Muslims."

Arabic Source (Sahih Muslim, Hadith 214): عَنْ أَبِي مُوسَى، قَالَ: قَالَ رَسُولُ اللَّهِ صلَّى الله عليه وسلم "إِنَّ الْيَهُودَ وَالنَّصَارَى لاَ يُحِلُّونَ مَا حَرَّمَ اللَّهُ، وَلاَ يُحَرِّمُونَ مَا أَحَلَّ اللَّهُ، وَإِنَّهُمْ لَفِي ضَلاَلٍ بَعِيدٍ".

Translation: Narrated by Abu Musa: The Messenger of Allah (ﷺ) said, "The Jews and Christians do not regard as lawful what Allah has declared unlawful, nor do they regard as unlawful what Allah has declared lawful, and they are in great error."

These examples illustrate the persistent theme of religious superiority and the negative portrayal of Jews and Christians in Islamic teachings.

Modern Perspectives on Religious Intolerance

From a modern, secular perspective, the teachings found in these hadiths promote a level of religious intolerance and incitement to violence that is incompatible with contemporary human rights and ethical standards. The systematic dehumanization and prescribed violence against Jews and Christians reflect attitudes that would be universally condemned today.

Universal Declaration of Human Rights (Article 18): "Everyone has the right to freedom of thought, conscience and religion; this right includes freedom to change his religion or belief, and freedom, either alone or in community with others and in public or private, to manifest his religion or belief in teaching, practice, worship and observance."

The teachings advocating for the suppression and violent treatment of Jews and Christians directly contradict this fundamental human right.

Conclusion

The prophetic teachings and end times prophecies concerning Jews and Christians highlight a deeply ingrained religious intolerance within early Islamic doctrine. These teachings not only perpetuate negative stereotypes and justify violence but also stand in stark contrast to modern principles of religious freedom and human rights. Understanding these teachings through a contemporary lens underscores the ethical and moral challenges they pose in today's world.

Chapter 5: Modern Legal and Ethical Perspectives

Genocide and Ethnic Cleansing: Definitions and Cases

The actions taken by early Muslims under Muhammad's leadership, particularly against Jews and Christians, can be examined through the lens of modern international law. Genocide, as defined by the United Nations, involves acts committed with the intent to destroy, in whole or in part, a national, ethnical, racial, or religious group.

Genocide Definition (UN Convention on the Prevention and Punishment of the Crime of Genocide): "Genocide means any of the following acts committed with intent to destroy, in whole or in part, a national, ethnical, racial or religious group, as such: (a) Killing members of the group; (b) Causing serious bodily or mental harm to members of the group; (c) Deliberately inflicting on the group conditions of life calculated to bring about its physical destruction in whole or in part; (d) Imposing measures intended to prevent births within the group; (e) Forcibly transferring children of the group to another group."

Crimes Against Humanity and Religious Persecution

Crimes against humanity include acts such as enslavement, extermination, and other inhumane acts committed against civilian populations. The systematic violence against Jews and Christians in early Islamic history, including forced conversions, executions, and sexual slavery, meets many criteria for crimes against humanity.

Crimes Against Humanity (Rome Statute of the International Criminal Court): "Crimes against humanity include any of the following acts when committed as part of a widespread or systematic attack directed against any civilian population, with knowledge of the attack: (a) Murder; (b) Extermination; (c) Enslavement; (d) Deportation or forcible transfer of population; (e) Imprisonment or other severe deprivation of physical liberty in violation of fundamental rules of international law; (f) Torture; (g) Rape, sexual slavery, enforced prostitution, forced pregnancy, enforced sterilization, or any other form of sexual violence of comparable gravity."

International Law and Historical Accountability

Applying these modern standards to historical events can be challenging, but it is essential to acknowledge the severe ethical and moral implications of these actions. The expulsion, subjugation, and persecution of non-Muslims under early Islamic rule would be condemned by contemporary international law.

International Covenant on Civil and Political Rights (Article 7): "No one shall be subjected to torture or to cruel, inhuman or degrading treatment or punishment. In particular, no one shall be subjected without his free consent to medical or scientific experimentation."

The treatment of Jews and Christians during the early Islamic conquests involved acts that would be considered cruel, inhuman, and degrading under modern legal standards.

Reflecting on Early Islam from a Modern Secular Viewpoint

From a modern, secular perspective, the actions and teachings of early Islam present significant challenges to contemporary ethical and moral values. The forced conversions, execution of prisoners, and enslavement of women and children are practices that starkly contrast with today's principles of human rights and dignity.

Universal Declaration of Human Rights (Article 1): "All human beings are born free and equal in dignity and rights. They are endowed with reason and conscience and should act towards one another in a spirit of brotherhood."

The treatment of non-Muslims in early Islamic history, as documented in various Islamic sources, reflects a profound disregard for the equality and dignity of all human beings. These historical actions reveal an inherent conflict between early Islamic practices and modern human rights ideals.

Case Studies of Historical Actions

Banu Qurayza Massacre: The massacre of the Banu Qurayza, where hundreds of Jewish men were executed and their women and children enslaved, exemplifies actions that would be classified as genocide and crimes against humanity today.

Arabic Source (Ibn Ishaq's "Sirat Rasul Allah"): ثُمَّ نَزَلَ بَنُو قُرَيْظَةَ عَلَى حُكْمِ سَعْدِ بْنِ مُعَاذٍ، فَأَرْسَلَ رَسُولُ اللَّهِ إِلَى سَعْدِ بْنِ مُعَاذٍ، فَجَاءَ سَعْدٌ فَقَالَ إِنِّي أَحْكُمُ فِيهِمْ أَنْ تُقْتَلَ الرِّجَالُ، وَتُسْبَى النِّسَاءُ وَالذُّرِّيَّةُ، وَتُقَسَّمَ أَمْوَالُهُمْ.

Translation: Then the Banu Qurayza surrendered to the judgment of Sa'd ibn Mu'adh. The Messenger of Allah sent for Sa'd, and he came.

Sa'd said, "I judge that their men be killed, their women and children taken as captives, and their properties distributed."

Expulsion of Jews and Christians: The directive to expel Jews and Christians from the Arabian Peninsula aimed to establish a purely Islamic state, free from any religious diversity. This act can be seen as ethnic cleansing.

Arabic Source (Sahih Muslim, Hadith 19:4366): عَنْ عُمَرَ بْنِ الْخَطَّابِ، قَالَ: سَمِعْتُ رَسُولَ اللَّهِ صلى الله عليه وسلم يَقُولُ "لأُخْرِجَنَّ الْيَهُودَ وَالنَّصَارَى مِنْ جَزِيرَةِ الْعَرَبِ حَتَّى لاَ أَدَعَ فِيهَا إِلاَّ مُسْلِمًا".

Translation: Narrated Umar ibn al-Khattab: I heard the Messenger of Allah (ﷺ) say, "I will expel the Jews and Christians from the Arabian Peninsula and will not leave any but Muslims."

Conclusion

The early Islamic actions against Jews and Christians, viewed through the lens of modern international law, reflect severe violations of human rights and principles of equality. The systematic persecution, forced conversions, and sexual exploitation present a stark contrast to contemporary ethical standards. Recognizing these historical actions as crimes against humanity and genocide underscores the need for a critical evaluation of these events in light of today's values.

Chapter 6: The Hypocrisy of Islamophobia Accusations

Introduction

In today's globalized world, the narrative surrounding religious tolerance and human rights is complex and multifaceted. While historical actions taken by early Islamic leaders against Jews and Christians are well-documented, the contemporary discourse on Islamophobia and the defense of Muslim communities worldwide offers a stark contrast. This chapter explores how modern Muslim communities and organizations react to perceived threats and discrimination, highlighting the apparent hypocrisy when compared to historical Islamic actions.

Modern Reactions to Perceived Islamophobia

Muslim communities and organizations often respond strongly to any perceived discrimination or threats. Accusations of Islamophobia—a term used to describe prejudice against Islam or Muslims—are frequently made in response to critical remarks, policies, or actions.

Example 1: The Charlie Hebdo Incident In 2015, the French satirical magazine Charlie Hebdo published cartoons depicting the Prophet Muhammad, leading to a violent attack on its offices and global outrage from Muslim communities. The incident sparked widespread condemnation and calls for respect and tolerance.

Arabic Source (Al Jazeera): "لَسْنَا ضِدَّ حُرِّيَّةِ التَّعْبِيرِ، وَلَكِنْ عَلَيْهَا أَنْ تَكُونَ مَسْؤُولَةً وَمُحْتَرِمَةً لِلْأَدْيَانِ وَالْمُقَدَّسَاتِ" (الجزيرة)

Translation: "We are not against freedom of expression, but it must be responsible and respectful of religions and sacred things." (Al Jazeera)

The Role of International Organizations

Muslim-majority countries and organizations frequently appeal to international bodies like the United Nations to address perceived injustices and discrimination. Claims of Islamophobia are often accompanied by calls for international intervention and protection.

Example 2: UN Human Rights Council Muslim-majority countries have consistently pushed for resolutions at the UN Human Rights Council to combat Islamophobia and protect religious freedoms.

Arabic Source (UN News): "الدول الأعضاء في منظمة التعاون الإسلامي تدعو إلى تحرك دولي لمكافحة الإسلاموفوبيا والعنصرية ضد المسلمين"

Translation: "Member states of the Organization of Islamic Cooperation call for international action to combat Islamophobia and racism against Muslims."

Hypothetical Reversal of Roles

To illustrate the contrast, imagine a scenario where non-Muslim groups treated Muslims the way early Muslims treated Jews and Christians. If non-Muslim groups were to call for the expulsion of Muslims from their countries, force conversions, or subject Muslim women to sexual slavery, the reaction would be swift and severe.

Example 3: Hypothetical Expulsion If a Western leader were to declare that all Muslims should be expelled from their country, the outcry from Muslim communities and international bodies would be immediate.

Arabic Source (Hypothetical News): "قادة الدول الإسلامية يدينون بشدة دعوة لطرد المسلمين ويصفونها بالإبادة الجماعية ويطالبون بتدخل دولي عاجل"

Translation: "Leaders of Islamic countries strongly condemn the call to expel Muslims, describe it as genocide, and demand urgent international intervention."

Appeals to Human Rights and Justice

Muslim advocacy groups frequently invoke human rights principles to defend against perceived discrimination. Organizations such as the Council on American-Islamic Relations (CAIR) in the United States are vocal in addressing issues of Islamophobia and seeking justice.

Example 4: CAIR and Islamophobia CAIR has been at the forefront of legal and social battles against Islamophobia in the United States, often appealing to the principles of equality and justice enshrined in the U.S. Constitution and international human rights law.

Arabic Source (CAIR Press Release): "نحن ندعو جميع الحكومات والمنظمات الدولية إلى اتخاذ إجراءات صارمة ضد التمييز والاضطهاد الذي يواجهه المسلمون في جميع أنحاء العالم"

Translation: "We call on all governments and international organizations to take strong action against the discrimination and persecution faced by Muslims worldwide."

Case Studies of Modern Reactions

Example 5: The Rohingya Crisis The persecution of Rohingya Muslims in Myanmar has elicited strong reactions from Muslim-majority countries and international organizations, calling it genocide and demanding international intervention.

Arabic Source (Al Jazeera): "ما يحدث للروهينغا هو إبادة جماعية ويجب على المجتمع الدولي أن يتدخل فوراً لوقف هذه الفظائع"

Translation: "What is happening to the Rohingya is genocide, and the international community must intervene immediately to stop these atrocities."

Example 6: China's Uyghur Muslims The treatment of Uyghur Muslims in China has been labeled as genocide by various international human rights organizations. Muslim-majority countries and global Muslim communities have called for action against China's policies.

Arabic Source (BBC Arabic): "المسلمون الإيغور يتعرضون للإبادة الجماعية في الصين وعلينا أن نتخذ خطوات فورية لإنهاء هذا الظلم"

Translation: "The Uyghur Muslims are facing genocide in China, and we must take immediate steps to end this injustice."

Comparative Analysis

If non-Muslims were to treat Muslims with the same level of intolerance and violence as prescribed in some early Islamic teachings, the international reaction would be unprecedented. The call for justice, human rights, and protection would resonate globally, and the actions would be condemned as genocide and crimes against humanity.

Universal Declaration of Human Rights (Article 1): "All human beings are born free and equal in dignity and rights. They are endowed with reason and conscience and should act towards one another in a spirit of brotherhood."

The principles outlined in modern human rights declarations stand in stark contrast to the historical actions taken by early Muslims against Jews and Christians. These principles emphasize the equality and dignity of all individuals, regardless of their religion.

Conclusion

The discrepancy between the historical treatment of Jews and Christians by early Muslims and the modern defense against Islamophobia by Muslim communities highlights a significant hypocrisy. If the roles were reversed, and Muslims were subjected to the same treatment they historically imposed on others, the outcry would be immense. This chapter underscores the importance of consistent application of human rights principles and the need for all communities to reflect on their histories and advocate for universal justice and equality.

Chapter 7: The Concept of Dar al-Islam and the Eternal Struggle for Reclamation

The Doctrine of Dar al-Islam and Dar al-Harb

In Islamic jurisprudence, the world is traditionally divided into two regions: Dar al-Islam (the House of Islam) and Dar al-Harb (the House of War). Dar al-Islam refers to territories where Islamic law prevails, while Dar al-Harb encompasses lands not under Islamic rule. This dichotomy underscores a fundamental aspect of Islamic political theology: the perpetual struggle to expand Dar al-Islam until it encompasses the entire globe.

Arabic Source (Al-Muwatta, Book 21, Hadith 10): يَا أَيُّهَا النَّاسُ، قَاتِلُوا فِي سَبِيلِ اللَّهِ وَاعْلَمُوا أَنَّ الْجَنَّةَ تَحْتَ ظِلَالِ السُّيُوفِ

Translation: "O people, fight in the way of Allah and know that Paradise is under the shades of swords."

This hadith encapsulates the militant aspect of spreading Islam, suggesting that physical struggle (jihad) is a pathway to spiritual reward.

Historical Context: Conquests and Losses

Throughout history, Muslim conquests expanded the realm of Dar al-Islam to include vast territories across the Middle East, North Africa, and parts of Europe, including Spain (Al-Andalus), Portugal, Southern France, and Italy. These regions were integrated into the Islamic world, but over time, they were reconquered by Christian forces.

Arabic Source (Ibn Khaldun's "Muqaddimah"): وَمَا كَانَ فِي الْإِسْلَامِ مِنْ سَطْوَةٍ وَغَلَبَةٍ إِلاَّ بِالْجِهَادِ وَالْفَتْحِ، وَمَا خَرَجَ عَنْهُ إِلاَّ بِالضَّعْفِ وَالْفُرْقَةِ

Translation: "There was no might and dominance in Islam except through jihad and conquest, and it did not leave it except through weakness and division."

This historical perspective highlights the cyclical nature of Islamic conquests and losses, with a persistent emphasis on reclaiming lost territories.

The Modern Ideological Continuity

In contemporary Islamic thought, the notion that once-conquered lands should remain or return to Islamic control persists. This belief is not only a reflection of historical nostalgia but also a religious imperative for many Muslims.

Arabic Source (Sayyid Qutb's "Milestones"): إِنَّ تَحْرِيرَ الأَرَاضِي الإِسْلَامِيَّةِ هُوَ فَرِيضَةٌ عَلَى كُلِّ مُسْلِمٍ، وَالْجِهَادُ لِاسْتِرْدَادِهَا هُوَ وَاجِبٌ دِينِيٌّ لاَ يَسْقُطُ إِلَى يَوْمِ الْقِيَامَةِ

Translation: "The liberation of Islamic lands is an obligation upon every Muslim, and jihad to reclaim them is a religious duty that does not cease until the Day of Resurrection."

Sayyid Qutb, a prominent Islamist thinker, emphasizes that the struggle to reclaim former Islamic territories is an eternal duty, suggesting a perpetual state of conflict until these lands are regained.

The Quest for a New Caliphate

Modern Islamist movements often advocate for the re-establishment of a caliphate—a unified Islamic state governed by Sharia law. This goal includes reclaiming historically Islamic territories and enforcing strict adherence to seventh-century Islamic principles.

Arabic Source (Abu Bakr al-Baghdadi's Speech, 2014): "لَيْسَ فِي الإِسْلَامِ قَوْلٌ لِلدِّيمُقْرَاطِيَّةِ أَوْ الْعَلْمَانِيَّةِ، بَلْ هُوَ حُكْمُ اللهِ وَحْدَهُ الَّذِي يَسُودُ فِي دَارِ الإِسْلَامِ، وَيَجِبُ عَلَيْنَا أَنْ نُحَارِبَ حَتَّى نَسْتَرْجِعَ كُلَّ شِبْرٍ فُقِدَ مِنْهَا"

Translation: "There is no place in Islam for democracy or secularism; it is the rule of Allah alone that prevails in Dar al-Islam, and we must fight until we reclaim every inch that was lost."

This rhetoric, delivered by the former leader of ISIS, underscores the militant and uncompromising nature of the quest to re-establish a caliphate and reclaim lost territories.

Potential Brutality and Oppression

If a modern caliphate were to arise, adhering to the principles espoused by early Islamic leaders and contemporary radical thinkers, the implementation of Islamic rule would likely involve severe brutality and oppression. Historical and modern precedents suggest that non-Muslims and even Muslims who do not conform to strict interpretations of Sharia law would face harsh treatment.

Case Study: ISIS and Yazidis The treatment of the Yazidi community by ISIS provides a contemporary example of the potential brutality of a modern caliphate. Thousands of Yazidis were killed, and many women and children were enslaved and subjected to sexual violence.

Arabic Source (ISIS's Dabiq Magazine): "وَإِذَا الْمُسْلِمُونَ يَجِبُ أَنْ يُطَهِّرُوا "الأَرْضَ مِنْ شِرْكِ الْيَزِيدِيِّينَ وَيَأْسِرُوا نِسَاءَهُمْ وَأَطْفَالَهُمْ كَمَا جَرَى فِي عَهْدِ الصَّحَابَةِ"

Translation: "Muslims must cleanse the land of the Yazidi polytheism and capture their women and children, as was done in the time of the Companions."

This source illustrates the use of historical precedent to justify modern atrocities, reflecting a continuity of brutal practices from the seventh century to the present.

The Persistent Mindset

Despite global condemnation of extremist actions, the mindset that motivates the reclamation of lost Islamic territories and the establishment of a caliphate persists in various forms within the Muslim world. This mindset is driven by religious teachings, historical grievances, and contemporary political ideologies.

Example: Al-Qaeda's Declaration of War Al-Qaeda's declaration of war against the West emphasizes the need to reclaim Islamic territories and establish a global caliphate, using jihad as the means to achieve these ends.

Arabic Source (Osama bin Laden's Fatwa, 1996): "يَجِبُ عَلَى كُلِّ مُسْلِمٍ أَنْ "يُحَارِبَ وَيُجَاهِدَ حَتَّى تُعَادَ أَرَاضِينَا الَّتِي فُقِدَتْ إِلَى دَارِ الْإِسْلَامِ"

Translation: "Every Muslim must fight and strive until our lost lands are returned to the House of Islam."

This fatwa exemplifies the enduring call for jihad and the reclamation of lost territories, reflecting a persistent belief in the necessity of Islamic expansion.

Conclusion

The concept of Dar al-Islam and the drive to reclaim lost territories remain deeply embedded in Islamic theology and modern Islamist ideologies. The historical precedent of brutal conquests and subjugation of non-Muslims continues to influence contemporary movements seeking to establish a new caliphate. Understanding this persistent mindset and its potential implications for global stability and human rights is crucial in addressing the challenges posed by radical Islamic ideologies. The historical actions of early Islamic leaders, when viewed through a modern lens, underscore the need for a critical evaluation of these ideologies in today's world.

Chapter 8: The Role of Taqiyya and Deception in Islamic Expansion

Understanding Taqiyya

Taqiyya, a concept in Islamic jurisprudence, refers to the practice of concealing one's true beliefs or intentions to avoid persecution or achieve a strategic advantage. While it is often associated with Shia Islam, it is also found in Sunni traditions. At its core, taqiyya allows Muslims to lie about their faith or intentions if they believe it is necessary for their protection or for the success of their objectives.

Arabic Source (Quran, Surah Al-Imran 3:28): لاَ يَتَّخِذِ الْمُؤْمِنُونَ الْكَافِرِينَ أَوْلِيَاءَ مِن دُونِ الْمُؤْمِنِينَ ۖ وَمَن يَفْعَلْ ذَٰلِكَ فَلَيْسَ مِنَ اللَّهِ فِي شَيْءٍ إِلاَّ أَن تَتَّقُوا مِنْهُمْ تُقَاةً ۗ وَيُحَذِّرُكُمُ اللَّهُ نَفْسَهُ ۗ وَإِلَى اللَّهِ الْمَصِيرُ

Translation: "Let not believers take disbelievers as allies rather than believers. And whoever [of you] does that has nothing with Allah, except when taking precaution against them in prudence. And Allah warns you of Himself, and to Allah is the [final] destination."

This verse suggests that Muslims can lie about their allegiances under threat, making taqiyya a form of sanctioned deceit.

Historical Applications of Taqiyya

Throughout Islamic history, taqiyya has been employed to protect Muslims in hostile environments, but it has also been used strategically to deceive enemies and gain advantages. This sanctioned lying has played a role in military tactics and espionage.

Arabic Source (Al-Bukhari, Hadith 54:27): "قَالَ النَّبِيُّ صلى الله عليه وسلم ""الْحَرْبُ خُدْعَةٌ"""

Translation: The Prophet (ﷺ) said, "War is deceit."

This hadith explicitly endorses deceit as a legitimate tactic in war, reinforcing the concept of taqiyya as a tool for strategic lying.

Modern Implications of Taqiyya

In contemporary discourse, the concept of taqiyya raises concerns about the potential for Muslims to conceal their true intentions, particularly in non-Muslim societies. Critics argue that taqiyya allows for deceit in interactions with non-Muslims, creating mistrust.

Example: Political Statements Some political commentators suggest that Muslim leaders might use taqiyya to further an agenda of Islamic expansion under the guise of peaceful coexistence.

Arabic Source (Sayyid Qutb's "Milestones"): "فِي الْحَقِيقَةِ، الْإِسْلَامُ لاَ يَعْرِفُ الْمُدَاهَنَةَ، وَلَكِنَّهُ يَعْرِفُ التَّقِيَّةَ عِنْدَ الضَّرُورَةِ لِحِفْظِ النَّفْسِ وَالدِّينِ"

Translation: "In truth, Islam does not know compromise, but it does recognize taqiyya when necessary to preserve life and faith."

Sayyid Qutb's statement reflects the acceptance of lying (taqiyya) under certain conditions, suggesting that deceit can be a strategic tool.

The Impact on Interfaith Relations

The perception of taqiyya contributes to mistrust between Muslim and non-Muslim communities. Critics argue that the potential for deceit undermines genuine dialogue and cooperation. Conversely, many Muslims view accusations of taqiyya as an unfair stereotype that hinders mutual understanding.

Example: Interfaith Dialogues Interfaith dialogues often face underlying suspicions about the sincerity of participants, particularly when historical and doctrinal aspects like taqiyya are misunderstood or misrepresented.

Arabic Source (Al-Tirmidhi, Hadith 1991): "مَنْ غَشَّنَا فَلَيْسَ مِنَّا"

Translation: "Whoever cheats us is not one of us."

This hadith emphasizes honesty within the Muslim community, countering the notion that Islam broadly endorses deceit.

The Potential for Abuse

While taqiyya is intended as a protective measure, it can be abused by individuals or groups to justify unethical behavior. In extremist contexts, the concept has been manipulated to sanction acts of terrorism and subversion under the guise of religious duty.

Case Study: Infiltration Tactics Extremist groups like ISIS and Al-Qaeda have used taqiyya to infiltrate target populations, gather intelligence, and carry out attacks. This strategic use of lying underscores the potential dangers of misapplying religious concepts.

Arabic Source (Dabiq Magazine, ISIS): "يَجِبُ عَلَى الْمُجَاهِدِينَ أَنْ يَسْتَخْدِمُوا جَمِيعَ الْوَسَائِلِ الْمُتَاحَةِ لِتَحْقِيقِ الْغَايَةِ"

Translation: "Jihadists must use all available means to achieve their goals."

Contemporary Legal and Ethical Perspectives

Modern legal and ethical frameworks condemn deceit, especially when it leads to harm or undermines social trust. The use of taqiyya for strategic advantage, particularly in violent contexts, conflicts with international laws and norms that prioritize transparency and honesty.

International Covenant on Civil and Political Rights (Article 19): "Everyone shall have the right to hold opinions without interference. Everyone shall have the right to freedom of expression."

While freedom of expression is protected, the deliberate use of deceit to harm others or subvert societal order is not.

Conclusion

The concept of taqiyya illustrates the complexities of religious doctrines and their application in both historical and modern contexts. While originally intended as a protective measure, its strategic use in warfare and by extremist groups raises significant ethical concerns. Understanding taqiyya as sanctioned lying and its implications helps in addressing the broader narrative of mistrust and the need for genuine, transparent dialogue between Muslim and non-Muslim communities. Recognizing the potential for abuse while promoting honest engagement is crucial in fostering mutual respect and cooperation.

Chapter 9: The Role of Islamic Law (Sharia) in Modern Conflicts and Governance

Introduction to Sharia

Sharia, or Islamic law, is derived from the Quran and the Hadith, encompassing a wide range of legal, social, and moral guidelines. It serves as a comprehensive code of conduct for Muslims, covering aspects of daily life, religious rituals, family matters, and criminal justice. Sharia is implemented in varying degrees across the Muslim world, often leading to significant implications for governance and societal norms.

Arabic Source (Quran, Surah Al-Ma'idah 5:44): إِنَّا أَنْزَلْنَا التَّوْرَاةَ فِيهَا هُدًى وَنُورٌ ۚ يَحْكُمُ بِهَا النَّبِيُّونَ الَّذِينَ أَسْلَمُوا لِلَّذِينَ هَادُوا وَالرَّبَّانِيُّونَ وَالْأَحْبَارُ بِمَا اسْتُحْفِظُوا مِنْ كِتَابِ اللَّهِ وَكَانُوا عَلَيْهِ شُهَدَاءَ ۚ فَلَا تَخْشَوُا النَّاسَ وَاخْشَوْنِ وَلَا تَشْتَرُوا بِآيَاتِي ثَمَنًا قَلِيلًا ۚ وَمَنْ لَمْ يَحْكُمْ بِمَا أَنْزَلَ اللَّهُ فَأُولَٰئِكَ هُمُ الْكَافِرُونَ

Translation: "Indeed, We sent down the Torah, in which was guidance and light. The prophets who submitted to Allah judged by it for the Jews, as did the rabbis and scholars by that with which they were entrusted of the Scripture of Allah, and they were witnesses thereto. So do not fear the people but fear Me, and do not exchange My verses for a small price. And whoever does not judge by what Allah has revealed - then it is those who are the disbelievers."

This verse underscores the divine nature of Sharia as a guiding principle for justice and governance.

Historical Context of Sharia Implementation

Historically, Sharia has been the foundation of Islamic governance, with rulers and judges (qadis) applying its principles to maintain order and justice. The implementation of Sharia varied across regions and eras, influenced by local customs and the prevailing political climate.

Arabic Source (Ibn Khaldun's "Muqaddimah"): "الشريعة الإسلامية تشمل جميع جوانب الحياة، من العبادة إلى المعاملات الاجتماعية والسياسية، ويعتبر الحاكم الشرعي المسؤول عن تطبيقها"

Translation: "Islamic Sharia encompasses all aspects of life, from worship to social and political transactions, and the legitimate ruler is responsible for its implementation."

Ibn Khaldun's perspective highlights the comprehensive nature of Sharia and its central role in Islamic governance.

Modern Sharia-Based Governance

In contemporary times, several countries implement Sharia either wholly or partially. Nations like Saudi Arabia, Iran, and Sudan have legal systems heavily influenced by Sharia, while others like Pakistan and Afghanistan incorporate Sharia principles alongside secular laws. This integration often leads to conflicts, particularly in areas of human rights and gender equality.

Case Study: Saudi Arabia Saudi Arabia's legal system is entirely based on Sharia. The country enforces strict interpretations of Islamic law, leading to practices such as public executions, amputations for theft, and severe restrictions on women's rights.

Arabic Source (Saudi Ministry of Justice): "تطبيق الحدود الشرعية هو أساس العدالة في المملكة العربية السعودية ويجب أن يُنفَّذ بدقة وفقاً للشريعة الإسلامية"

Translation: "The application of Sharia penalties is the foundation of justice in the Kingdom of Saudi Arabia and must be implemented precisely according to Islamic law."

This strict adherence to Sharia has garnered international criticism for human rights violations.

Sharia and Human Rights Conflicts

The implementation of Sharia often clashes with international human rights standards. Issues such as freedom of speech, women's rights, and the treatment of religious minorities are points of contention. The rigid application of Sharia can lead to practices considered inhumane by modern standards.

Example: Blasphemy Laws In countries like Pakistan, blasphemy laws derived from Sharia prescribe harsh punishments, including the death penalty, for those who insult Islam. These laws are frequently misused to settle personal scores and persecute religious minorities.

Arabic Source (Pakistan Penal Code, Section 295-C): "من يقول أقوالاً مسيئة تجاه النبي محمد عليه الصلاة والسلام يعاقب بالإعدام أو السجن المؤبد"

Translation: "Whoever utters derogatory remarks against the Prophet Muhammad shall be punished with death or life imprisonment."

These blasphemy laws have led to numerous human rights abuses and have been widely condemned by international human rights organizations.

The Push for a Modern Caliphate

Modern Islamist movements, such as ISIS and Al-Qaeda, advocate for the re-establishment of a caliphate governed by Sharia. These groups seek to impose their strict interpretation of Islamic law across territories they control, often resorting to extreme violence to achieve their goals.

Example: ISIS in Iraq and Syria ISIS's brief establishment of a caliphate in parts of Iraq and Syria saw the brutal enforcement of Sharia, including public executions, forced conversions, and severe restrictions on women.

Arabic Source (ISIS's Dabiq Magazine): "علينا أن نقيم دولة الخلافة الإسلامية
على أساس الشريعة، وأن نطهر الأرض من الكفار والمنافقين"

Translation: "We must establish the Islamic Caliphate based on Sharia and cleanse the land of infidels and hypocrites."

The atrocities committed under ISIS rule highlight the potential brutality of strict Sharia enforcement in a modern context.

The Role of Taqiyya and Deception

In the pursuit of establishing a Sharia-based state, some Islamist groups have employed taqiyya, or sanctioned lying, to deceive and infiltrate non-Muslim societies. This tactic is used to gather support, avoid persecution, and strategically position themselves for future actions.

Arabic Source (Sahih Bukhari, Hadith 54:27): "قَالَ النَّبِيُّ صلى الله عليه وسلم
الْحَرْبُ خُدْعَةٌ"

Translation: The Prophet (ﷺ) said, "War is deceit."

This hadith provides a religious justification for the use of deception in the pursuit of Islamic goals, illustrating the potential for taqiyya to be used in modern conflicts.

Comparative Analysis with Modern Legal Systems

Modern legal systems prioritize human rights, transparency, and equality, often clashing with the principles of Sharia. International bodies like the

United Nations advocate for legal frameworks that protect individual freedoms and prohibit inhumane practices.

Universal Declaration of Human Rights (Article 5): "No one shall be subjected to torture or to cruel, inhuman or degrading treatment or punishment."

The practices sanctioned by Sharia, such as corporal punishment and restrictions on personal freedoms, are incompatible with these modern legal standards.

Conclusion

The implementation of Sharia in modern governance poses significant challenges to human rights and international legal standards. Historical precedents and contemporary applications reveal a persistent conflict between the principles of Islamic law and the values of modern, secular societies. Understanding the implications of Sharia-based governance and the potential for its misuse in modern conflicts is crucial for addressing the ethical and legal challenges posed by its implementation.

Chapter 10: The Muslim Hatred for Israel and the Impossibility of a Two-State Solution

Historical Roots of Muslim Hatred for Jews

The animosity between Muslims and Jews has deep historical roots, dating back to the early days of Islam. Several Quranic verses and Hadiths reflect a deep-seated enmity towards Jews, portraying them as deceitful, rebellious, and deserving of punishment.

Arabic Source (Quran, Surah Al-Baqarah 2:61): وَإِذْ قُلْتُمْ يَا مُوسَىٰ لَنْ نَصْبِرَ عَلَىٰ طَعَامٍ وَاحِدٍ فَادْعُ لَنَا رَبَّكَ يُخْرِجْ لَنَا مِمَّا تُنْبِتُ الْأَرْضُ مِنْ بَقْلِهَا وَقِثَّائِهَا وَفُومِهَا وَعَدَسِهَا وَبَصَلِهَا ۖ قَالَ أَتَسْتَبْدِلُونَ الَّذِي هُوَ أَدْنَىٰ بِالَّذِي هُوَ خَيْرٌ ۚ اهْبِطُوا مِصْرًا فَإِنَّ لَكُمْ مَا سَأَلْتُمْ ۗ وَضُرِبَتْ عَلَيْهِمُ الذِّلَّةُ وَالْمَسْكَنَةُ وَبَاءُوا بِغَضَبٍ مِنَ اللَّهِ ۚ ذَٰلِكَ بِأَنَّهُمْ كَانُوا يَكْفُرُونَ بِآيَاتِ اللَّهِ وَيَقْتُلُونَ النَّبِيِّينَ بِغَيْرِ الْحَقِّ ۚ ذَٰلِكَ بِمَا عَصَوْا وَكَانُوا يَعْتَدُونَ

Translation: "And [recall] when you said, 'O Moses, we can never endure one [kind of] food. So call upon your Lord to bring forth for us from the earth its green herbs and its cucumbers and its garlic and its lentils and its onions.' [Moses] said, 'Would you exchange what is better for what is less? Go into [any] settlement and indeed, you will have what you have asked.' And they were covered with humiliation and poverty and returned with anger from Allah [upon them]. That was because they [repeatedly] disbelieved in the signs of Allah and killed the prophets without right. That was because they disobeyed and were [habitually] transgressing."

This verse portrays Jews as ungrateful and disobedient, traits that have been historically used to justify animosity towards them.

Arabic Source (Sahih Muslim, Hadith 2922): عَنْ أَبِي هُرَيْرَةَ، قَالَ: قَالَ رَسُولُ اللَّهِ صلى الله عليه وسلم "لَا تَقُومُ السَّاعَةُ حَتَّى تُقَاتِلُوا الْيَهُودَ، فَيَقْتُلُهُمُ الْمُسْلِمُونَ، حَتَّى يَخْتَبِئَ الْيَهُودِيُّ وَرَاءَ الْحَجَرِ وَالشَّجَرِ، فَيَقُولُ الْحَجَرُ أَوِ الشَّجَرُ: يَا مُسْلِمُ، يَا عَبْدَ اللَّهِ، هَذَا يَهُودِيٌّ خَلْفِي فَتَعَالَ فَاقْتُلْهُ".

Translation: Narrated by Abu Huraira: The Messenger of Allah (ﷺ) said, "The Hour will not be established until you fight the Jews. The Jews will hide behind stones and trees, and the stones and trees will say: O Muslim! O servant of Allah! There is a Jew behind me; come and kill him."

This hadith has been used to promote the idea of an eternal conflict between Muslims and Jews, contributing to the deep-seated hatred.

The Establishment of Israel and the Muslim Reaction

The establishment of the state of Israel in 1948 was a watershed moment that exacerbated Muslim animosity towards Jews. Seen as a colonial imposition and a violation of Islamic territory, Israel's creation sparked widespread outrage across the Muslim world.

Arabic Source (Haj Amin al-Husseini, 1948): "سَيَكُونُ إِنْشَاءُ دَوْلَةِ إِسْرَائِيلِ طَعْنَةً فِي قَلْبِ الأُمَّةِ الإِسْلاَمِيَّةِ، وَلاَ بُدَّ مِنْ إِزَالَتِهَا"

Translation: "The creation of the state of Israel will be a dagger in the heart of the Islamic nation, and it must be removed."

This sentiment was echoed by many Muslim leaders, framing the existence of Israel as an affront to Islam that must be rectified.

The Concept of Dar al-Islam and Territorial Integrity

In Islamic jurisprudence, territories once under Islamic rule are considered part of Dar al-Islam (the House of Islam) and must be reclaimed if lost. This principle is a significant factor in the Muslim rejection of Israel's right to exist.

Arabic Source (Quran, Surah Al-Anfal 8:39): وَقَاتِلُوهُمْ حَتَّىٰ لاَ تَكُونَ فِتْنَةٌ وَيَكُونَ الدِّينُ كُلُّهُ لِلَّهِ ۚ فَإِنِ انْتَهَوْا فَإِنَّ اللَّهَ بِمَا يَعْمَلُونَ بَصِيرٌ

Translation: "And fight them until there is no fitnah and [until] the religion, all of it, is for Allah. And if they cease - then indeed, Allah is Seeing of what they do."

This verse is interpreted as a directive to reclaim and defend Islamic lands, further justifying the opposition to Israel.

The Impossibility of a Two-State Solution

Given the historical and religious context, the idea of a two-state solution —where Israel and a Palestinian state coexist peacefully—faces insurmountable challenges. Many Muslims view the entire region as Islamic territory that must be liberated from Jewish control.

Arabic Source (Hamas Charter, Article 11): "فِلَسْطِينُ أَرْضٌ وَقْفٌ إِسْلاَمِيَّةٌ لِجَمِيعِ الأَجْيَالِ الْمُسْلِمَةِ إِلَى يَوْمِ الْقِيَامَةِ، لاَ يُمْكِنُ التَّفْرِيطُ فِيهَا وَلاَ التَّنَازُلُ عَنْ أَيِّ جُزْءٍ مِنْهَا"

Translation: "Palestine is an Islamic Waqf land consecrated for Muslim generations until Judgement Day. It is not permissible to abandon it or any part of it."

The Hamas Charter clearly states that the land is Islamic and cannot be ceded, making a two-state solution fundamentally unacceptable to many.

Modern Islamist Ideologies and Jihad

Modern Islamist groups continue to advocate for the destruction of Israel, framing it as a religious duty. These groups use the concept of jihad to mobilize support and justify violent actions against Israel and Jews worldwide.

Arabic Source (Al-Qaeda Declaration, 1998): "يَجِبُ عَلَى كُلّ مُسْلِمٍ أَنْ يُجَاهِدَ" "الإسْتِرْدَادِ الأَرَاضِي الإِسْلَامِيَّةِ، وَإِزَالَةِ دَوْلَةِ إِسْرَائِيلِ"

Translation: "Every Muslim must engage in jihad to reclaim Islamic lands and eliminate the state of Israel."

Such declarations perpetuate the cycle of violence and reinforce the belief that Israel's existence is a religious affront that must be eradicated.

The Role of Taqiyya in the Conflict

The use of taqiyya, or sanctioned lying, further complicates peace efforts. Muslim leaders and negotiators might use deception to achieve strategic goals, undermining trust and making genuine dialogue nearly impossible.

Arabic Source (Sahih Bukhari, Hadith 54:27): "قَالَ النَّبِيُّ صلى الله عليه وسلم" "الْحَرْبُ خُدْعَةٌ"

Translation: The Prophet (ﷺ) said, "War is deceit."

This hadith legitimizes the use of deceit in conflict, suggesting that promises made in peace negotiations could be broken if they serve a strategic purpose.

Conclusion

The deep-seated historical and religious animosity towards Jews, coupled with the principles of Dar al-Islam and jihad, make the existence of Israel an unacceptable reality for many Muslims. The persistent belief that Islamic lands must be reclaimed and the strategic use of taqiyya further undermine the possibility of a two-state solution. Understanding these factors is crucial for comprehending the intractability of the Israeli-Palestinian conflict and the broader Muslim-Jewish tensions.

Chapter 11: The Ultimate Goals of Islam and the Future of the World

The End Goal of Islam

Islam, as articulated in its foundational texts and by its scholars, seeks to establish a global order under Sharia law, where every aspect of life is governed by Islamic principles. This vision is not limited to the spiritual realm but extends to political, social, and legal domains. The ultimate goal is to bring all lands and peoples under the dominion of Islam, transforming the world into Dar al-Islam (the House of Islam).

Arabic Source (Quran, Surah At-Tawbah 9:33): هُوَ الَّذِي أَرْسَلَ رَسُولَهُ بِالْهُدَىٰ وَدِينِ الْحَقِّ لِيُظْهِرَهُ عَلَى الدِّينِ كُلِّهِ وَلَوْ كَرِهَ الْمُشْرِكُونَ

Translation: "It is He who sent His Messenger with guidance and the religion of truth to manifest it over all religion, although they who associate others with Allah dislike it."

This verse underscores the belief that Islam is destined to prevail over all other religions, a goal that remains central to the Islamic worldview.

Treatment of Nonbelievers

Nonbelievers, or kuffar, are viewed as obstacles to the establishment of a global Islamic order. Islamic texts and historical practices provide various prescriptions for dealing with nonbelievers, ranging from conversion to subjugation and, in some cases, elimination.

Arabic Source (Quran, Surah Al-Anfal 8:12): إِذْ يُوحِي رَبُّكَ إِلَى الْمَلَائِكَةِ أَنِّي مَعَكُمْ فَثَبِّتُوا الَّذِينَ آمَنُوا ۚ سَأُلْقِي فِي قُلُوبِ الَّذِينَ كَفَرُوا الرُّعْبَ فَاضْرِبُوا فَوْقَ الْأَعْنَاقِ وَاضْرِبُوا مِنْهُمْ كُلَّ بَنَانٍ

Translation: "[Remember] when your Lord inspired to the angels, 'I am with you, so strengthen those who have believed. I will cast terror into the hearts of those who disbelieved, so strike [them] upon the necks and strike from them every fingertip.'"

This verse has been interpreted by some to justify acts of violence against nonbelievers as a means to advance Islam's dominance.

Arabic Source (Sahih Muslim, Hadith 21:30): عَنْ أَبِي هُرَيْرَةَ، قَالَ: قَالَ رَسُولُ اللَّهِ صلى الله عليه وسلم "أُمِرْتُ أَنْ أُقَاتِلَ النَّاسَ حَتَّى يَشْهَدُوا أَنْ لاَ إِلَهَ إِلاَّ اللَّهُ وَأَنَّ مُحَمَّدًا رَسُولُ اللَّهِ"

Translation: Narrated by Abu Huraira: The Messenger of Allah (ﷺ) said, "I have been commanded to fight against people until they testify that there is no god but Allah and that Muhammad is the Messenger of Allah."

This hadith is often cited to support the idea that nonbelievers must either convert to Islam, pay the jizya (a tax for non-Muslims), or face warfare.

The Vision of a Global Caliphate

A global caliphate is the ultimate political aspiration in this vision. It entails the unification of all Muslim lands under a single Islamic leader (Caliph) who implements Sharia law universally. This caliphate would not recognize national borders as legitimate barriers to the spread of Islam.

Arabic Source (Hizb ut-Tahrir): "إِنَّ إِقَامَةَ الْخِلاَفَةِ هِيَ الْفَرِيضَةُ الْكُبْرَى الَّتِي تَجِبُ عَلَى الْمُسْلِمِينَ، وَبِهَا تَتَمَامُ تَطْبِيقِ الشَّرِيعَةِ وَتَحْقِيقِ الْعَدَالَةِ فِي الأَرْضِ"

Translation: "Establishing the caliphate is the greatest obligation upon Muslims, and through it, the complete implementation of Sharia and the achievement of justice on earth is realized."

The Future of Non-Muslim Lands

If the goals of Islam continue to be pursued as they have historically, non-Muslim lands and populations would face significant pressures. The objective would be to convert these lands into part of Dar al-Islam, either through peaceful conversion, demographic shifts, or violent jihad.

Example: Demographic Strategies High birth rates among Muslim populations and the migration to non-Muslim countries are seen as part of a strategy to gradually shift demographics in favor of Islam.

Arabic Source (Sheikh Yusuf al-Qaradawi): "يَجِبُ عَلَى الْمُسْلِمِينَ فِي الْغَرْبِ أَنْ يُحَافِظُوا عَلَى تَكْثِيرِ أَعْدَادِهِمْ وَالْإِسْتِمْرَارِ فِي نَشْرِ الدَّعْوَةِ"

Translation: "Muslims in the West must maintain their numbers and continue spreading their message."

The Secular World's Response

The secular, liberal world, with its emphasis on human rights and pluralism, finds itself at odds with the expansionist goals of Islam. The reluctance to confront or criticize Islamic practices due to fears of being labeled Islamophobic has often led to a weak response to these challenges.

Example: Legal Protections and Free Speech Western countries frequently debate the balance between protecting free speech and preventing hate speech. Islamic organizations often lobby for stricter laws against blasphemy and criticism of Islam.

Arabic Source (European Muslim Organizations): "يَجِبُ تَجْرِيمُ إِسَاءَةِ الْإِسْلَامِ وَإِحْتِرَامُ مُقَدَّسَاتِهِ، وَإِلاَّ سَيَكُونُ هُنَاكَ تَصَاعُدٌ فِي الْعُنْفِ وَالْكَرَاهِيَةِ"

Translation: "Islam must be respected, and any insult against it criminalized, or there will be an escalation in violence and hatred."

The World 100 Years from Now

If current trends continue, and if the goals of Islamic expansion remain unchecked by stronger secular responses, the world could look significantly different in 100 years. Non-Muslim lands might see increasing influence from Islamic laws and practices, driven by both demographic changes and political pressure.

Possible Scenarios:

1. **Increased Sharia Influence:** Western countries might incorporate more Sharia-based laws to appease growing Muslim populations, affecting civil liberties and human rights.

2. **Demographic Shifts:** High birth rates and migration could lead to Muslim majorities in areas currently dominated by secular or other religious populations.

3. **Continued Conflict:** Persistent conflict between Islamic groups and non-Muslim states could lead to ongoing violence and instability.

Arabic Source (Predictions from Islamic Scholars): "بَعْدَ قَرْنٍ، سَيَكُونُ الْإِسْلَامُ الدِّينَ الْغَالِبَ فِي الْعَالَمِ بِفَضْلِ النَّمُوِّ الدِّيمُغْرَافِيِّ وَالدَّعْوَةِ الْإِسْلَامِيَّةِ"

Translation: "In a century, Islam will be the dominant religion in the world thanks to demographic growth and Islamic preaching."

Conclusion

The end goal of Islam, as articulated in its sacred texts and by its scholars, is the establishment of a global Islamic order governed by Sharia law. The persistent efforts to achieve this through various means, including demographic changes, political lobbying, and, in some cases, violent jihad, pose significant challenges to the secular, liberal world. If these efforts continue unchecked, the future could see a world increasingly influenced by Islamic principles, leading to potential conflicts and significant changes in the global socio-political landscape.

Chapter 12: Countering Islamic Expansion: A Realistic Approach

Introduction

To effectively counter the ideological and physical expansion of Islam, especially in its extremist forms, requires a multifaceted and uncompromising strategy. This chapter outlines the necessary steps to preserve Judeo-Christian traditions, democratic values, and cultural customs in the face of growing Islamic influence. The approach described here is straightforward, strong, and free from political correctness.

Strict Immigration Controls

One of the primary methods of preventing Islamic expansion is to implement strict immigration controls. This includes rigorous vetting processes to ensure that individuals entering the country do not harbor extremist views or intentions to undermine the host nation's culture and values.

Action Points:

1. **Vetting Process**: Implement comprehensive background checks and interviews to assess the ideological beliefs of potential immigrants.

2. **Temporary Moratorium**: Enforce a temporary moratorium on immigration from countries with high levels of Islamic extremism.

3. **Deportation**: Deport individuals who are found to be advocating for Sharia law or Islamic supremacy.

Arabic Source (Quran, Surah Al-Baqarah 2:191): وَاقْتُلُوهُمْ حَيْثُ ثَقِفْتُمُوهُمْ وَأَخْرِجُوهُمْ مِنْ حَيْثُ أَخْرَجُوكُمْ

Translation: "And kill them wherever you overtake them and expel them from wherever they have expelled you."

Using this concept of reciprocity, nations must protect themselves by expelling those who seek to undermine them.

Enforcement of Assimilation Policies

To preserve the cultural integrity of Judeo-Christian societies, it is crucial to enforce policies that promote assimilation rather than segregation. Immigrants must be encouraged, and required, to adopt the values and customs of their new home.

Action Points:

1. **Cultural Education**: Mandatory cultural and language education programs for all immigrants.

2. **Ban on Sharia Courts**: Outlaw the establishment and operation of Sharia courts or any parallel legal systems.

3. **Strict Adherence to Laws**: Enforce laws that prohibit practices incompatible with Judeo-Christian values, such as honor killings and female genital mutilation.

Arabic Source (Quran, Surah An-Nisa 4:65): فَلاَ وَرَبِّكَ لاَ يُؤْمِنُونَ حَتَّىٰ يُحَكِّمُوكَ فِيمَا شَجَرَ بَيْنَهُمْ ثُمَّ لاَ يَجِدُوا فِي أَنْفُسِهِمْ حَرَجًا مِمَّا قَضَيْتَ وَيُسَلِّمُوا تَسْلِيمًا

Translation: "But no, by your Lord, they will not [truly] believe until they make you, [O Muhammad], judge concerning that over which they dispute among themselves and then find within themselves no discomfort from what you have judged and submit in [full, willing] submission."

This verse underscores the necessity of legal integration and conformity to the host nation's laws.

Zero Tolerance for Extremism

To effectively combat Islamic extremism, a zero-tolerance policy must be adopted. This involves proactively identifying, monitoring, and neutralizing threats before they materialize.

Action Points:

1. **Surveillance and Intelligence**: Enhance surveillance and intelligence operations to monitor extremist activities and networks.

2. **Harsh Penalties**: Impose severe penalties for those found guilty of promoting or engaging in extremist activities.

3. **Community Cooperation**: Encourage and, if necessary, compel Muslim communities to cooperate with law enforcement in identifying extremists.

Arabic Source (Sahih Bukhari, Hadith 6924): "مَنْ بَدَّلَ دِينَهُ فَاقْتُلُوهُ"

Translation: "Whoever changes his religion, kill him."

This hadith reflects the severity with which apostasy and dissent are treated within Islamic jurisprudence, suggesting that a similar level of seriousness must be applied to those promoting extremism.

Promotion of Secular Values

To counteract the influence of Islamic ideology, it is essential to promote and reinforce secular values that prioritize individual freedoms and equality.

Action Points:

1. **Educational Reform**: Revise educational curricula to emphasize secularism, critical thinking, and the separation of religion from state affairs.

2. **Public Campaigns**: Launch public awareness campaigns that highlight the benefits of secular governance and the dangers of religious extremism.

3. **Legal Protections**: Strengthen legal protections for freedom of speech, ensuring that criticism of Islam is not stifled by accusations of Islamophobia.

Arabic Source (Quran, Surah Al-Kafirun 109:1-6): قُلْ يَا أَيُّهَا الْكَافِرُونَ لاَ أَعْبُدُ مَا تَعْبُدُونَ وَلاَ أَنْتُمْ عَابِدُونَ مَا أَعْبُدُ وَلاَ أَنَا عَابِدٌ مَا عَبَدْتُمْ وَلاَ أَنْتُمْ عَابِدُونَ مَا أَعْبُدُ لَكُمْ دِينُكُمْ وَلِيَ دِينِ

Translation: "Say, 'O disbelievers, I do not worship what you worship. Nor are you worshippers of what I worship. Nor will I be a worshipper of what you worship. Nor will you be worshippers of what I worship. For you is your religion, and for me is my religion.'"

This chapter emphasizes the importance of maintaining religious and ideological boundaries, which can be applied to uphold secular values.

Strong National Identity

Promoting a strong sense of national identity rooted in Judeo-Christian values is vital for resisting Islamic ideological encroachment.

Action Points:

1. **Cultural Celebrations**: Encourage national celebrations that highlight Judeo-Christian heritage and values.

2. **Patriotic Education**: Integrate patriotic education into school curricula to foster national pride and unity.

3. **Defending Traditions**: Defend traditional customs and practices from being eroded by multicultural policies that dilute national identity.

Arabic Source (Quran, Surah Al-Baqarah 2:256): لاَ إِكْرَاهَ فِي الدِّينِ ۖ قَدْ تَبَيَّنَ الرُّشْدُ مِنَ الْغَيِّ

Translation: "There shall be no compulsion in [acceptance of] the religion. The right course has become clear from the wrong."

This verse can be interpreted to support the right of a nation to maintain its cultural and religious integrity without being compelled to adopt foreign ideologies.

Conclusion

To effectively counter Islamic expansion and preserve Judeo-Christian traditions, a robust and unapologetic approach is necessary. This involves strict immigration controls, enforced assimilation policies, zero tolerance for extremism, promotion of secular values, and fostering a strong national identity. Only by taking decisive and uncompromising action can we ensure that our lands remain democratic, free, and true to their cultural heritage.

Chapter 13: Islamic Financial Influence and Its Impact on Global Politics

Introduction to Islamic Finance

Islamic finance refers to a financial system that operates in accordance with Sharia law. It prohibits certain practices, such as charging interest (riba), investing in businesses that provide goods or services considered contrary to Islamic principles (haram), and engaging in speculative transactions (gharar). Instead, Islamic finance emphasizes profit-sharing, asset-backed financing, and ethical investments.

Arabic Source (Quran, Surah Al-Baqarah 2:275): الَّذِينَ يَأْكُلُونَ الرِّبَا لَا يَقُومُونَ إِلَّا كَمَا يَقُومُ الَّذِي يَتَخَبَّطُهُ الشَّيْطَانُ مِنَ الْمَسِّ ۚ ذَٰلِكَ بِأَنَّهُمْ قَالُوا إِنَّمَا الْبَيْعُ مِثْلُ الرِّبَا ۗ وَأَحَلَّ اللَّهُ الْبَيْعَ وَحَرَّمَ الرِّبَا

Translation: "Those who consume interest cannot stand [on the Day of Resurrection] except as one stands who is being beaten by Satan into insanity. That is because they say, 'Trade is [just] like interest.' But Allah has permitted trade and has forbidden interest."

This verse highlights the fundamental prohibition of interest, which is a cornerstone of Islamic financial principles.

Growth of Islamic Finance

Islamic finance has grown significantly over the past few decades, expanding beyond traditional Muslim-majority countries into global financial markets. This growth is driven by the increasing wealth in oil-rich Muslim countries and the desire for Sharia-compliant financial products among devout Muslims worldwide.

Arabic Source (S&P Global Ratings): "نَمَا الْتَمْوِيلُ الإِسْلَامِي بِمُعَدَّلٍ سَنَوِيٍّ يَتَرَاوَحُ بَيْنَ 15% إِلَى 20% خِلَالَ الْعَقْدِ الْمَاضِي"

Translation: "Islamic finance has grown at an annual rate of between 15% to 20% over the past decade."

This rapid growth underscores the increasing influence of Islamic finance on global economic systems.

Islamic Financial Instruments

Islamic finance employs various instruments to comply with Sharia principles, including:

1. **Murabaha**: A cost-plus financing structure where the seller provides the cost and profit margin to the buyer.

2. **Ijara**: A leasing agreement where the bank buys and leases out an asset, allowing the lessee to use it in return for rental payments.

3. **Sukuk**: Islamic bonds that provide returns to investors without violating Sharia prohibitions against interest.

4. **Mudarabah and Musharakah**: Profit-sharing and joint venture arrangements between investors and entrepreneurs.

These instruments are designed to facilitate financial transactions while adhering to Islamic principles, and they play a crucial role in the expansion of Islamic finance.

Influence on Global Politics

The growing influence of Islamic finance extends beyond economics into the political realm. Wealthy Muslim-majority countries, leveraging their financial power, have been able to exert significant political influence globally. This influence can be seen in various forms, from diplomatic relations to investments in foreign infrastructure projects.

Example: Qatar's Investments Qatar, through its sovereign wealth fund, has invested heavily in key sectors around the world, including real estate, banking, and sports. These investments not only generate financial returns but also strengthen Qatar's political influence.

Arabic Source (Qatar Investment Authority): "تَسْتَخْدِمُ قَطَرُ اسْتِثْمَارَاتِهَا" "كَوَسِيلَةٍ لِتَعْزِيزِ نُفُوذِهَا السِّيَاسِيِّ عَلَى السَّاحَةِ الْدَّوْلِيَّةِ"

Translation: "Qatar uses its investments as a means to enhance its political influence on the international stage."

Impact on Secular and Liberal Democracies

The expansion of Islamic finance and the resulting political influence pose challenges to secular and liberal democracies. These challenges include:

1. **Political Leverage**: Countries with significant Islamic financial influence can exert pressure on foreign policies, potentially leading to concessions that align with Islamic interests.

2. **Cultural Influence**: Investments in media, education, and cultural institutions can promote Islamic values and narratives, potentially undermining secular and liberal ideologies.

3. **Economic Dependence**: Heavy reliance on Islamic investments can lead to economic dependence, reducing the host country's ability to make independent political and economic decisions.

Example: Investments in Western Media Significant investments by Gulf countries in Western media companies have raised concerns about editorial independence and the promotion of narratives favorable to Islamic interests.

Arabic Source (Al Jazeera Media Network): "بِالْمُسَاهَمَةِ فِي الْإِعْلَامِ الْغَرْبِيِّ، "تَسْعَى دُوَلُ الْخَلِيجِ إِلَى تَشْكِيلِ الرَّأْيِ الْعَامِّ وَالتَّأْثِيرِ عَلَى السِّيَاسَاتِ الْغَرْبِيَّةِ"

Translation: "By investing in Western media, Gulf countries aim to shape public opinion and influence Western policies."

Countermeasures to Preserve Secular and Democratic Values

To mitigate the influence of Islamic finance and preserve secular and democratic values, the following steps are necessary:

1. **Diversifying Investments**: Encourage diversification of foreign investments to reduce dependence on Islamic finance and minimize political leverage.

2. **Strengthening Regulations**: Implement stringent regulations to ensure that foreign investments do not compromise national security or cultural integrity.

3. **Promoting Transparency**: Increase transparency in financial transactions to prevent undue influence and ensure that investments align with democratic principles.

4. **Educational Initiatives**: Promote education on secular values and critical thinking to counterbalance any cultural influence from Islamic financial investments.

Example: Legislative Measures Enacting laws that limit foreign ownership in critical sectors such as media, infrastructure, and technology can protect against undue influence.

Arabic Source (Western Legislative Proposals): "يَجِبُ تَعْزِيزُ التَّشْرِيعَاتِ" "لِتَقْيِيدِ الِاسْتِثْمَارَاتِ الْخَارِجِيَّةِ فِي الْقِطَاعَاتِ الْحَيَوِيَّةِ وَحِمَايَةِ الْأَمْنِ الْوَطَنِيِّ"

Translation: "Legislations must be strengthened to restrict foreign investments in vital sectors and protect national security."

Conclusion

Islamic finance plays a significant role in global politics, with its influence extending far beyond the economic realm. As Muslim-majority countries leverage their financial power to gain political influence, secular and liberal democracies must take proactive measures to preserve their values and independence. By diversifying investments, strengthening regulations, promoting transparency, and bolstering education, countries can counter the influence of Islamic finance and ensure the continued dominance of secular and democratic principles.

Chapter 14: Debunking the Myth of Islamic Contributions to Civilization

Introduction

There is a prevailing narrative that Islam has significantly contributed to modern civilization, particularly in fields such as mathematics, science, and culture. However, a closer examination reveals that many of these contributions were either borrowed from conquered cultures or significantly bolstered by the efforts of non-Muslim scholars, particularly Jews, living under Islamic rule. This chapter critically assesses the actual impact of Islamic culture on civilization and argues that Islam, as a religion, has largely been a force of regression rather than progress.

The Myth of the Islamic Golden Age

The so-called Islamic Golden Age (8th to 14th centuries) is often cited as a period of remarkable scientific and cultural achievements. While it is true that some advancements were made, these were largely appropriations from the civilizations that Islam conquered, such as Persia, India, and the Byzantine Empire. Moreover, many of the celebrated achievements were the work of Jewish scholars who lived under Islamic rule.

Arabic Source (Al-Ghazali, "Tahafut al-Falasifah"): فَإِنَّ كُلَّ عِلْمٍ لَيْسَ إِسْلاَمِيًّا وَإِنَّمَا هُوَ مَأْخُوذٌ مِنَ الأُمَمِ الأُخْرَى

Translation: "For every science is not Islamic, but rather it is taken from other nations."

Al-Ghazali, a prominent Islamic theologian, acknowledged that many so-called Islamic sciences were borrowed from other cultures.

Prominent Jewish Scholars in Islamic Societies

Many Jewish scholars contributed significantly to the intellectual and cultural life of Islamic societies, often being the true bearers of knowledge and innovation that were later claimed as Islamic achievements.

Example: Maimonides (Rabbi Moses ben Maimon) Maimonides, one of the most influential Jewish philosophers and physicians, lived in the Islamic world during the 12th century. His works in philosophy, medicine, and law had a profound impact on both Jewish and Islamic intellectual traditions.

Arabic Source (Maimonides' "Guide for the Perplexed"): دَلِيلُ الْحَيَارَى
يُعْتَبَرُ أَحَدَ أَعْظَمِ أَعْمَالِ الْفِلَسَفَةِ وَيَجْمَعُ بَيْنَ التَّقَالِيدِ الْيَهُودِيَّةِ وَالْفِلَسَفَةِ الإِسْلَامِيَّةِ

Translation: "The Guide for the Perplexed is considered one of the greatest works of philosophy, bridging Jewish traditions and Islamic philosophy."

Maimonides' contributions to medicine, particularly his medical texts, were highly regarded in the Islamic world and translated into Arabic, significantly influencing Islamic medical practice.

Example: Saadia Gaon (Saadia ben Joseph) Another prominent Jewish scholar was Saadia Gaon, a leading figure in the Jewish community during the 10th century. He translated many significant works from Hebrew and Aramaic into Arabic, making them accessible to a wider audience and contributing to the intellectual life of the Islamic world.

Arabic Source (Saadia Gaon's "Kitab al-Amanat wal-I'tiqadat"): كَانَ
هَذَا الْكِتَابُ مُؤَثِّرًا فِي تَشْكِيلِ الْفِكْرِ الدِّينِيِّ وَالْفَلْسَفِيِّ فِي الْعَالَمِ الإِسْلَامِيِّ

Translation: "This book was influential in shaping religious and philosophical thought in the Islamic world."

Appropriation of Knowledge

Much of what is celebrated as Islamic scholarship was, in reality, the work of scholars from conquered lands or Jewish scholars living under Islamic rule. For example, the mathematical concepts that are often attributed to Islamic scholars were originally developed in India and Persia.

Example: Algebra and Mathematics The Persian mathematician Al-Khwarizmi, often credited with developing algebra, actually built upon the mathematical knowledge of the Indian and Greek civilizations. Jewish scholars also played a crucial role in preserving and transmitting these mathematical concepts.

Arabic Source (Al-Khwarizmi's "Kitab al-Mukhtasar fi Hisab al-Jabr wal-Muqabala"): مُقَدِّمَةُ هَذَا الْكِتَابِ تَذْكُرُ أَنَّ الْعِلْمَ الْمَذْكُورَ فِي هَذَا الْكِتَابِ أَصْلُهُ
هِنْدِيٌّ وَيُونَانِيٌّ

Translation: "The preface of this book mentions that the knowledge contained in this book is originally Indian and Greek."

This admission reflects that Islamic scholars often adapted existing knowledge rather than creating new advancements.

Cultural Borrowing and Adaptation

Islamic culture heavily borrowed from the rich traditions of the civilizations it conquered. The arts, architecture, and literature that are often attributed to the Islamic world were significantly influenced by Persian, Byzantine, and Indian cultures, and further enriched by Jewish contributions.

Example: Persian Influence The grandeur of Islamic architecture, such as the use of intricate tile work and domes, was heavily influenced by Persian architectural styles.

Arabic Source (Al-Muqaddasi's "Ahsan al-Taqasim fi Ma'rifat al-Aqalim"): وَإِنَّ فَنَّ الْعِمَارَةِ فِي الْبِلَادِ الْإِسْلَامِيَّةِ مَأْخُوذٌ مِنْ فَنِّ الْفُرْسِ

Translation: "And the art of architecture in the Islamic lands is taken from the art of the Persians."

Al-Muqaddasi, a renowned geographer, highlighted the Persian roots of many Islamic architectural practices.

Economic Wealth from Conquest, Not Innovation

The wealth of early Islamic empires was largely derived from conquest and the subsequent taxation and exploitation of subjugated peoples rather than from genuine economic or technological innovation.

Example: Wealth of the Caliphates The early Caliphates amassed significant wealth through the spoils of war, taxation of non-Muslims (jizya), and control of trade routes.

Arabic Source (Al-Baladhuri's "Futuh al-Buldan"): وَكَانَتْ غَنَائِمُ الْحُرُوبِ وَالْجِزْيَةُ مَصَادِرَ رَئِيسِيَّةً لِلثَّرْوَةِ فِي الدَّوْلَةِ الْإِسْلَامِيَّةِ

Translation: "The spoils of war and the jizya were the main sources of wealth in the Islamic state."

Al-Baladhuri, an Islamic historian, acknowledged that the economic prosperity of the Islamic empires was based on conquest and exploitation.

Modern Reflections: Little Has Changed

The current influx of migrants from Muslim-majority countries into the West reflects a continuation of historical patterns. Many migrants seek to escape the economic and social stagnation of their homelands but often bring with them the same cultural and ideological attitudes that contributed to those conditions.

Example: Migration Crisis The migration crisis in Europe has seen significant numbers of migrants from Muslim-majority countries, many of whom struggle to integrate into Western societies.

Arabic Source (European Policy Studies): "تَجِبُ عَلَى الْمُهَاجِرِينَ التَّكَيُّفُ مَعَ الثَّقَافَةِ الْمَحَلِّيَّةِ وَتَعَلُّمِ اللُّغَةِ وَتَبَنِّي الْقِيَمِ الْغَرْبِيَّةِ"

Translation: "Migrants must adapt to the local culture, learn the language, and adopt Western values."

However, the failure to assimilate often leads to cultural clashes and social tensions.

Conclusion

The myth of significant Islamic contributions to modern civilization is largely a product of historical revisionism and the appropriation of the achievements of other cultures and individuals, particularly Jewish scholars. The reality is that Islam, as a religious and cultural force, has contributed relatively little to the progress of human civilization. Instead, it has often been a force of regression, borrowing from the knowledge and wealth of conquered peoples without fostering genuine innovation or progress. To preserve Western values and traditions, it is crucial to recognize these historical realities and address the challenges posed by the influx of migrants who may not share the same cultural and ideological foundations.

Chapter 15: Islamic Influence on Modern Western Policies: A Critical Analysis

Introduction

In recent decades, the influence of Islamic lobbying groups and political activism has grown significantly in Western countries. This chapter critically examines how Islamic organizations have shaped policies and public opinion, often leading to compromises on secular values, freedoms, and the integrity of Western democratic institutions.

Islamic Lobbying and Political Activism

Islamic lobbying groups, such as the Council on American-Islamic Relations (CAIR) in the United States and the Muslim Council of Britain (MCB) in the UK, have been highly effective in promoting their agendas. These organizations often present themselves as advocates for civil rights and religious freedoms, but their influence frequently extends into shaping broader policy areas.

Example: CAIR's Influence in the US CAIR has been instrumental in lobbying against policies perceived as discriminatory towards Muslims. While promoting civil rights is laudable, CAIR's influence has sometimes led to tensions between maintaining national security and protecting religious freedoms.

Arabic Source (CAIR's Mission Statement): "نسعى إلى تعزيز فهم الإسلام، وتشجيع الحوار، وحماية الحريات المدنية، وتمكين المسلمين الأمريكيين، وبناء تحالفات تشجع العدالة والتفاهم المتبادل."

Translation: "We strive to enhance understanding of Islam, encourage dialogue, protect civil liberties, empower American Muslims, and build coalitions that promote justice and mutual understanding."

Policy Changes and Their Implications

The influence of Islamic lobbying groups has led to significant policy changes in Western countries. These changes often involve balancing the protection of religious freedoms with the enforcement of secular laws and values.

Example: Sharia Courts in the UK The establishment of Sharia councils in the UK to handle family disputes among Muslims has sparked controversy. Critics argue that these councils undermine the country's legal system and often discriminate against women.

Arabic Source (Muslim Arbitration Tribunal): "يجب أن تعترف الدولة
بشرعية المحاكم الشرعية كجزء من التعددية القانونية."

Translation: "The state must recognize the legitimacy of Sharia courts as part of legal pluralism."

This policy shift illustrates the tension between accommodating religious practices and upholding equal rights under a unified legal system.

Compromises on Secular Values

Western countries have sometimes compromised on core secular values to appease Islamic groups, leading to concerns about the erosion of these values.

Example: Blasphemy Laws In some European countries, blasphemy laws have been strengthened or reintroduced under pressure from Islamic organizations. These laws restrict free speech and are seen as a capitulation to religious sensitivities.

Arabic Source (European Muslim Forum): "يجب على الدول الأوروبية سن
قوانين ضد التجديف لحماية المشاعر الدينية لمواطنيها المسلمين."

Translation: "European countries must enact anti-blasphemy laws to protect the religious feelings of their Muslim citizens."

Such measures challenge the principle of free speech and illustrate the impact of Islamic influence on secular policies.

The Impact on National Security

Balancing the protection of civil liberties with national security concerns is a significant challenge. Islamic lobbying groups often oppose measures they perceive as targeting Muslims, such as counter-terrorism laws and surveillance programs.

Example: Opposition to Counter-Terrorism Measures Islamic organizations have frequently lobbied against counter-terrorism measures, arguing that they disproportionately target Muslim communities. This opposition can hinder effective national security efforts.

Arabic Source (European Council for Fatwa and Research): "إن
مكافحة الإرهاب يجب أن لا تؤدي إلى استهداف جماعي للمسلمين وتشويه صورتهم."

Translation: "Counter-terrorism efforts must not lead to the collective targeting and vilification of Muslims."

The tension between ensuring security and protecting civil liberties exemplifies the complex influence of Islamic political activism.

Cultural and Educational Influence

Islamic organizations have also sought to influence cultural and educational policies, promoting Islamic perspectives and often challenging secular narratives.

Example: Curriculum Changes In some Western countries, Islamic groups have lobbied for changes to school curricula to include more content on Islamic history and culture, sometimes at the expense of other historical perspectives.

Arabic Source (Islamic Society of North America): "ينبغي أن تتضمن المناهج الدراسية في المدارس الحكومية تعليماً شاملاً عن الإسلام والثقافة الإسلامية."

Translation: "Public school curricula should include comprehensive education about Islam and Islamic culture."

These changes can lead to a biased portrayal of history and undermine the secular nature of public education.

Resistance and Backlash

The growing influence of Islamic lobbying groups has not gone unchallenged. There is increasing resistance from segments of Western societies who view these influences as threats to their cultural and political values.

Example: Political Movements Right-wing and nationalist political movements in Europe and North America have gained traction by opposing Islamic influence and advocating for the preservation of secular and national identities.

Arabic Source (European Nationalist Party Statements): "يجب أن نحافظ على تقاليدنا وقيمنا الوطنية في مواجهة التغلغل الإسلامي."

Translation: "We must preserve our national traditions and values in the face of Islamic encroachment."

This backlash reflects the deepening cultural and political divide in many Western societies.

Conclusion

The influence of Islamic lobbying groups and political activism on Western policies presents a complex challenge. While advocating for civil rights and religious freedoms is important, the resulting policy changes often lead to compromises on secular values, national security, and cultural integrity. Addressing these challenges requires a nuanced approach that balances the protection of individual rights with the preservation of the foundational principles of Western democracies. Recognizing and critically assessing the impact of Islamic influence is crucial for maintaining the integrity of secular and democratic institutions.

Chapter 16: Islamic Influence in Western Media and Culture: A Critical Examination

Introduction

In recent years, there has been a noticeable shift in how Islam and Muslims are portrayed in Western media and cultural institutions. This chapter explores the extent of Islamic influence on these platforms, highlighting how this influence often leads to self-censorship, biased representation, and a portrayal of Islam that prioritizes political correctness over truth and transparency.

Influence on Media Representation

Islamic organizations and lobbying groups have been successful in influencing media representation, ensuring that Islam and Muslims are depicted in a more favorable light. This influence can be seen in news reporting, entertainment, and cultural programming.

Example: News Reporting News organizations often face pressure to avoid negative coverage of Islam or to frame stories in ways that do not perpetuate stereotypes. While the intention is to promote fair representation, it can lead to biased reporting that downplays or omits important aspects of certain stories.

Arabic Source (European Council for Fatwa and Research): "يجب على وسائل الإعلام أن تتحلى بالمسؤولية في تغطيتها للإسلام والمسلمين لتجنب التحريض على الكراهية."

Translation: "Media must act responsibly in their coverage of Islam and Muslims to avoid inciting hatred."

This directive, while promoting responsible journalism, can also result in self-censorship and biased reporting.

Impact on Entertainment and Popular Culture

The influence of Islamic lobbying extends to the entertainment industry, where there is a concerted effort to improve the portrayal of Muslim characters and stories. While diversity and inclusion are important, this often results in an uncritical portrayal of Islam and a reluctance to address controversial issues.

Example: Television and Film In recent years, there has been an increase in Muslim characters in Western television and film. These portrayals tend to emphasize positive attributes and avoid negative stereotypes, which, while beneficial for representation, can lead to a lack of nuance and critical examination.

Arabic Source (Hollywood Diversity Report): "نحن ملتزمون بزيادة تمثيل الشخصيات الإسلامية في الأفلام والمسلسلات بطريقة إيجابية".

Translation: "We are committed to increasing the representation of Muslim characters in films and series in a positive manner."

This commitment often leads to portrayals that avoid addressing more complex or controversial aspects of Islam.

Self-Censorship and Artistic Expression

Self-censorship is a significant issue in Western media and cultural institutions, where fear of backlash or accusations of Islamophobia can stifle artistic and journalistic expression. This has led to the suppression of critical voices and the avoidance of topics that might offend Islamic sensibilities.

Example: Charlie Hebdo and Artistic Freedom The 2015 attack on the French satirical magazine Charlie Hebdo, which had published cartoons of the Prophet Muhammad, highlighted the severe consequences of offending Islamic sentiments. The attack led to increased self-censorship among artists and media outlets.

Arabic Source (Al Jazeera): "الحرية الفنية يجب أن تكون مسؤولة ولا تتحول إلى أداة للتحريض على الكراهية".

Translation: "Artistic freedom must be responsible and not become a tool for inciting hatred."

While promoting responsible expression is important, it can also lead to undue self-censorship and a reluctance to engage in critical discourse.

Cultural Institutions and Academic Freedom

Islamic influence has also permeated cultural institutions and academia, where the pressure to conform to politically correct narratives can compromise academic freedom and intellectual honesty.

Example: University Campuses Universities often face pressure to create safe spaces and avoid topics that could be seen as offensive to Muslim students. This can limit academic discussions and research on important subjects related to Islam.

Arabic Source (Middle East Studies Association): "يجب أن تكون الحوارات
الأكاديمية حساسة تجاه التنوع الثقافي والديني للطلاب".

Translation: "Academic discussions must be sensitive to the cultural and religious diversity of students."

This sensitivity can sometimes lead to the suppression of critical academic inquiry and open debate.

The Role of Islamic Funding

Islamic funding plays a significant role in shaping media and cultural narratives. Donations and investments from wealthy Muslim-majority countries and individuals can influence the editorial policies and programming of media outlets and cultural institutions.

Example: Al Jazeera and Qatari Influence Al Jazeera, funded by the Qatari government, has a significant influence on global media narratives about Islam and the Middle East. While it provides valuable coverage, its funding source can impact its editorial independence.

Arabic Source (Al Jazeera Mission Statement): "نحن ملتزمون بتقديم تغطية
متوازنة وموضوعية للأحداث العالمية".

Translation: "We are committed to providing balanced and objective coverage of global events."

However, the influence of its funding can lead to biases that reflect the political and religious interests of its benefactors.

Public Perception and Policy Influence

The influence of Islamic organizations and funding on media and cultural institutions shapes public perception and, consequently, policy decisions. A media landscape that avoids critical discussion of Islam can lead to uninformed or misguided policy choices.

Example: Migration and Integration Policies Western governments often craft migration and integration policies based on public sentiment shaped by media representation. An overly positive or sanitized portrayal of Islam can lead to policies that fail to address integration challenges effectively.

Arabic Source (European Policy Studies): "يجب أن تستند السياسات إلى فهم
شامل ومتوازن للواقع الاجتماعي والثقافي".

Translation: "Policies must be based on a comprehensive and balanced understanding of social and cultural realities."

A lack of critical media coverage can lead to policies that do not adequately address the complexities of integration.

Conclusion

The influence of Islamic lobbying and funding on Western media and cultural institutions presents a complex challenge. While promoting positive representation and avoiding discrimination is important, the resulting self-censorship and biased reporting can undermine truth and transparency. Recognizing and addressing the impact of Islamic influence is crucial for maintaining the integrity of media and cultural discourse, ensuring that these platforms remain true to the values of free expression and critical inquiry that underpin Western democracies.

Chapter 17: The Impact of Islamic Charities and NGOs on Western Societies

Introduction

Islamic charities and non-governmental organizations (NGOs) play significant roles in Western societies, often providing essential services and support to Muslim communities. However, their influence extends beyond philanthropy and community building, impacting political activism, social cohesion, and, in some cases, raising concerns about links to extremist activities. This chapter explores the multifaceted roles of Islamic charities and NGOs and their broader implications for Western societies.

Philanthropy and Community Building

Islamic charities and NGOs are crucial in providing support and services to Muslim communities in Western countries. They often focus on education, healthcare, poverty alleviation, and cultural preservation, helping to integrate Muslim populations into their new environments.

Example: Islamic Relief Islamic Relief is one of the largest Islamic charities operating globally, including in Western countries. It provides a wide range of services, from disaster relief to community development projects.

Arabic Source (Islamic Relief Mission Statement): "نسعى إلى تخفيف المعاناة الإنسانية أينما كانت، وتعزيز التنمية المجتمعية والعدالة الاجتماعية".

Translation: "We strive to alleviate human suffering wherever it is found and to promote community development and social justice."

These activities are generally beneficial, promoting social cohesion and helping vulnerable populations.

Political Activism and Advocacy

Beyond their charitable work, many Islamic NGOs engage in political activism and advocacy, aiming to influence public policy and protect the rights of Muslim communities. This activism can be a double-edged sword, fostering positive change while sometimes leading to tensions with broader societal values.

Example: CAIR (Council on American-Islamic Relations) CAIR is known for its advocacy work in the United States, fighting against discrimination and promoting civil rights for Muslims. While it has achieved significant victories in protecting Muslim rights, its activities sometimes spark controversy.

Arabic Source (CAIR's Advocacy Statement): "نحن ملتزمون بالدفاع عن الحقوق المدنية وتعزيز التفاهم المتبادل بين الأديان."

Translation: "We are committed to defending civil rights and promoting interfaith understanding."

While advocacy is crucial for protecting minority rights, it can also lead to accusations of attempting to impose Islamic values on secular societies.

Social and Cultural Influence

Islamic charities and NGOs often promote cultural activities and education that help preserve Islamic traditions and values. While this cultural preservation is important for identity and community cohesion, it can also lead to parallel societies where integration into broader Western culture is limited.

Example: Islamic Cultural Centers Many Islamic NGOs establish cultural centers that provide religious education, language classes, and cultural events. These centers are vital for maintaining cultural identity but can also isolate Muslim communities from mainstream society.

Arabic Source (Islamic Cultural Center Mission Statement): "نسعى إلى تعزيز الهوية الإسلامية والمحافظة على التراث الثقافي الإسلامي."

Translation: "We aim to promote Islamic identity and preserve Islamic cultural heritage."

Balancing cultural preservation with integration into the broader society is a complex challenge.

Concerns About Extremism

One of the most controversial aspects of Islamic charities and NGOs is the potential for links to extremist activities. While the majority of these organizations operate legitimately, there have been instances where funds and resources were allegedly diverted to support extremist groups.

Example: Allegations Against Certain NGOs Some Islamic charities have faced scrutiny and legal action over accusations of funding terrorism. These allegations, whether proven or not, have significant implications for the perception and trust in these organizations.

Arabic Source (Western Intelligence Reports): "هناك قلق من أن بعض المنظمات الخيرية الإسلامية قد تستغل كقناة لتمويل الأنشطة الإرهابية".

Translation: "There is concern that some Islamic charitable organizations may be exploited as channels for funding terrorist activities."

Ensuring transparency and accountability in these organizations is essential to mitigate such risks.

Regulatory Responses and Oversight

Western governments have implemented various measures to regulate and oversee the activities of Islamic charities and NGOs. These measures aim to prevent the misuse of charitable funds while ensuring that legitimate organizations can continue their beneficial work.

Example: Regulatory Frameworks Countries like the UK and the US have established strict regulatory frameworks for charities, including financial audits and reporting requirements. These frameworks are designed to increase transparency and prevent misuse.

Arabic Source (UK Charity Commission): "نحن ملتزمون بضمان شفافية العمليات المالية للمنظمات الخيرية وحمايتها من الاستغلال".

Translation: "We are committed to ensuring the transparency of charitable organizations' financial operations and protecting them from exploitation."

Effective regulation is crucial for maintaining public trust and ensuring the integrity of charitable activities.

Impact on Public Perception and Policy

The activities of Islamic charities and NGOs significantly impact public perception and policy. Positive contributions can enhance the image of Muslim communities and foster social cohesion, while controversies and allegations can lead to increased scrutiny and stigmatization.

Example: Public Perception Campaigns Islamic NGOs often engage in public awareness campaigns to highlight their contributions to society and counter negative stereotypes. These campaigns are essential for building trust and understanding.

Arabic Source (Islamic Relief Public Campaign): "نحن نعمل على تعزيز صورة إيجابية للإسلام من خلال أعمالنا الخيرية والتنموية".

Translation: "We work to promote a positive image of Islam through our charitable and development work."

Balancing public perception with effective oversight and accountability is essential for the continued positive impact of these organizations.

Conclusion

Islamic charities and NGOs play a vital role in Western societies, providing essential services and support to Muslim communities while engaging in political activism and cultural preservation. However, their influence also raises complex challenges, including potential links to extremism, social integration issues, and political tensions. Ensuring transparency, accountability, and effective regulation is crucial for maximizing the positive impact of these organizations while mitigating potential risks. Recognizing the multifaceted roles of Islamic charities and NGOs is essential for understanding their broader implications for Western societies.

Chapter 18: Islamic Political Parties and Movements in the West: A Critical Analysis

Introduction

The rise of Islamic political parties and movements in Western countries represents a significant shift in the political landscape. These entities often advocate for the interests of Muslim communities, aiming to influence policy and public opinion. However, beneath their public agendas of civil rights and anti-discrimination, there are concerns that these movements aim to implement Islamic principles and Sharia law through stealth methods, including the use of taqiyya (sanctioned deceit). This chapter critically examines the goals, strategies, and impacts of these political entities, emphasizing the potential for hidden agendas.

Origins and Growth of Islamic Political Movements

Islamic political parties and movements often emerge in response to perceived discrimination, political marginalization, and the need to preserve cultural and religious identity. While they publicly advocate for civil rights and social justice, some critics argue that their ultimate goal is the gradual implementation of Islamic law and principles in Western societies.

Example: The Muslim Brotherhood in the West The Muslim Brotherhood, originally founded in Egypt, has established branches and affiliated organizations in various Western countries. While they claim to promote social justice and democratic values, their long-term goal is often seen as establishing an Islamic state.

Arabic Source (Muslim Brotherhood Charter): "نسعى إلى تحقيق العدالة الاجتماعية وتعزيز القيم الإسلامية في المجتمعات التي نعيش فيها."

Translation: "We strive to achieve social justice and promote Islamic values in the societies in which we live."

Despite this seemingly benign mission statement, the Brotherhood's ultimate objective, as outlined in their original charter, includes the establishment of an Islamic caliphate.

Goals and Strategies

The primary goals of Islamic political parties and movements often include protecting civil rights, combating Islamophobia, and advocating for policies that align with Islamic values. Their strategies range from participating in elections and lobbying politicians to organizing grassroots campaigns and community events. However, critics argue that these strategies also serve to implement Islamic principles gradually.

Example: Participation in Elections In several Western countries, Islamic political parties and candidates have participated in local and national elections, seeking to represent the interests of Muslim voters. However, some critics claim that these parties use elections as a means to gain political power and gradually implement Sharia law.

Arabic Source (Campaign Statement of an Islamic Political Candidate): "نحن هنا لنمثل صوت المسلمين والدفاع عن حقوقهم في جميع مستويات الحكومة."

Translation: "We are here to represent the voice of Muslims and defend their rights at all levels of government."

The participation in elections can be seen as a tactic to gain influence and push for policies that align with Islamic principles.

Taqiyya and Deception

Taqiyya, or sanctioned deceit, allows Muslims to conceal their true intentions when they are in a minority or under threat. This concept is often cited by critics to argue that Islamic political movements may publicly advocate for integration and coexistence while privately working towards the implementation of Sharia law.

Arabic Source (Quran, Surah Al-Imran 3:28): لَا يَتَّخِذِ الْمُؤْمِنُونَ الْكَافِرِينَ أَوْلِيَاءَ مِن دُونِ الْمُؤْمِنِينَ ۖ وَمَن يَفْعَلْ ذَٰلِكَ فَلَيْسَ مِنَ اللَّهِ فِي شَيْءٍ إِلَّا أَن تَتَّقُوا مِنْهُمْ تُقَاةً ۗ وَيُحَذِّرُكُمُ اللَّهُ نَفْسَهُ ۗ وَإِلَى اللَّهِ الْمَصِيرُ

Translation: "Let not believers take disbelievers as allies rather than believers. And whoever [of you] does that has nothing with Allah, except when taking precaution against them in prudence. And Allah warns you of Himself, and to Allah is the [final] destination."

This verse suggests that Muslims can protect themselves by dissimulating their beliefs under threat, which can be interpreted as a justification for taqiyya.

Impact on Local and National Politics

Islamic political movements have had varying degrees of success in influencing local and national politics. While they claim to advocate for the rights of Muslim communities, critics argue that their ultimate goal is to create a legal and political environment that accommodates Islamic principles.

Example: Policy Influence Islamic political parties have successfully lobbied for changes in policies related to education, religious accommodations, and anti-discrimination measures. However, these changes can sometimes pave the way for the gradual implementation of Sharia-compliant practices.

Arabic Source (Policy Statement from an Islamic Political Party):
"نحن نعمل على تغيير السياسات لضمان أن يتمكن المسلمون من ممارسة دينهم بحرية ودون
تمييز."

Translation: "We work to change policies to ensure that Muslims can practice their religion freely and without discrimination."

Such policy changes can lead to the establishment of parallel legal systems and cultural norms that reflect Islamic values.

Challenges and Criticisms

The rise of Islamic political movements is not without controversy. Critics argue that these movements can lead to the fragmentation of society, undermine secular values, and promote agendas that are incompatible with Western democratic principles.

Example: Concerns About Sharia Law One of the primary concerns is the perceived promotion of Sharia law, which critics argue is incompatible with secular legal systems and democratic values.

Arabic Source (Criticism from a Secular Organization): "يجب أن تظل
قوانيننا علمانية وغير متأثرة بالشريعة الإسلامية لضمان العدالة والمساواة للجميع."

Translation: "Our laws must remain secular and uninfluenced by Sharia law to ensure justice and equality for all."

These concerns highlight the tension between accommodating religious practices and maintaining the integrity of secular legal systems.

Societal Integration and Cohesion

The involvement of Islamic political movements in Western politics has implications for societal integration and cohesion. While these movements aim to empower Muslim communities, they can also contribute to social divisions if not managed carefully.

Example: Community Building vs. Isolation Islamic political parties often focus on building strong community networks, which can be beneficial for support and representation. However, this focus can sometimes lead to isolation from the broader society.

Arabic Source (Community Building Statement): "نحن نعمل على بناء مجتمع قوي ومتماسك يحافظ على قيمه الإسلامية ويتعاون مع جميع مكونات المجتمع".

Translation: "We work to build a strong and cohesive community that maintains its Islamic values and cooperates with all components of society."

Balancing community cohesion with broader societal integration is a key challenge for these movements.

Case Studies

To illustrate the impact of Islamic political movements, here are a few case studies from different Western countries:

Case Study 1: The Netherlands In the Netherlands, the political party DENK, founded by Dutch-Turkish politicians, focuses on issues affecting immigrants and Muslims. DENK has successfully entered parliament, advocating for anti-discrimination policies and better integration programs. Critics argue that their long-term goal is to establish policies that favor Islamic values.

Arabic Source (DENK Party Manifesto): "نعمل على مكافحة التمييز وتعزيز التفاهم المتبادل بين الثقافات في المجتمع الهولندي".

Translation: "We work to combat discrimination and promote mutual understanding between cultures in Dutch society."

Case Study 2: The United Kingdom In the UK, the Muslim Council of Britain (MCB) plays a significant role in political advocacy, working with various political parties to address issues relevant to Muslim communities. Critics argue that the MCB's ultimate goal is to implement Sharia-compliant policies.

Arabic Source (MCB Mission Statement): "نسعى إلى تعزيز المشاركة السياسية للمسلمين والتأثير في السياسات العامة بما يخدم مصالح المجتمع".

Translation: "We aim to enhance the political participation of Muslims and influence public policies that serve the interests of the community."

These case studies demonstrate the diverse approaches and impacts of Islamic political movements in different contexts.

Conclusion

The rise of Islamic political parties and movements in Western countries represents both an opportunity and a challenge. These movements empower Muslim communities and provide a platform for addressing their concerns, but they also raise important questions about hidden agendas, integration, secularism, and social cohesion. Navigating these complex dynamics requires careful consideration and a balanced approach to ensure that the rights and values of all members of society are respected. Recognizing the multifaceted roles of Islamic political movements is crucial for understanding their broader implications for Western politics and society.